100 MANDALA COLORING BOOK

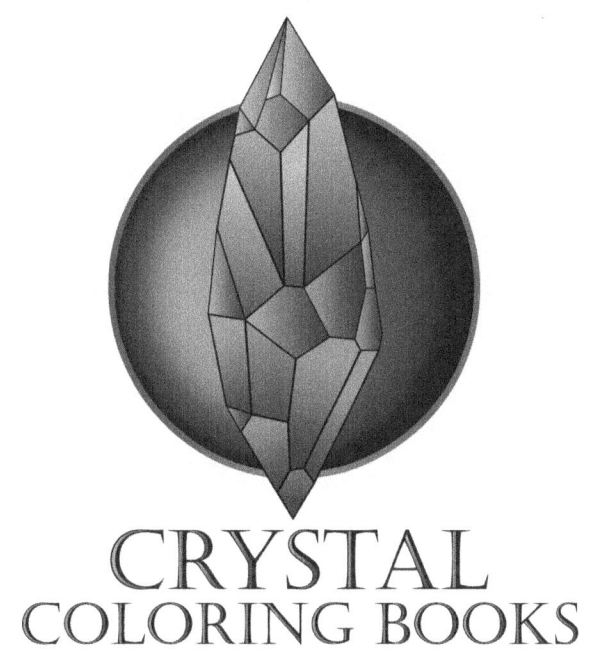

CRYSTAL
COLORING BOOKS

Copyright © 2020 Crystal Coloring Books

All rights Reserved.
ISBN: 9798646893735

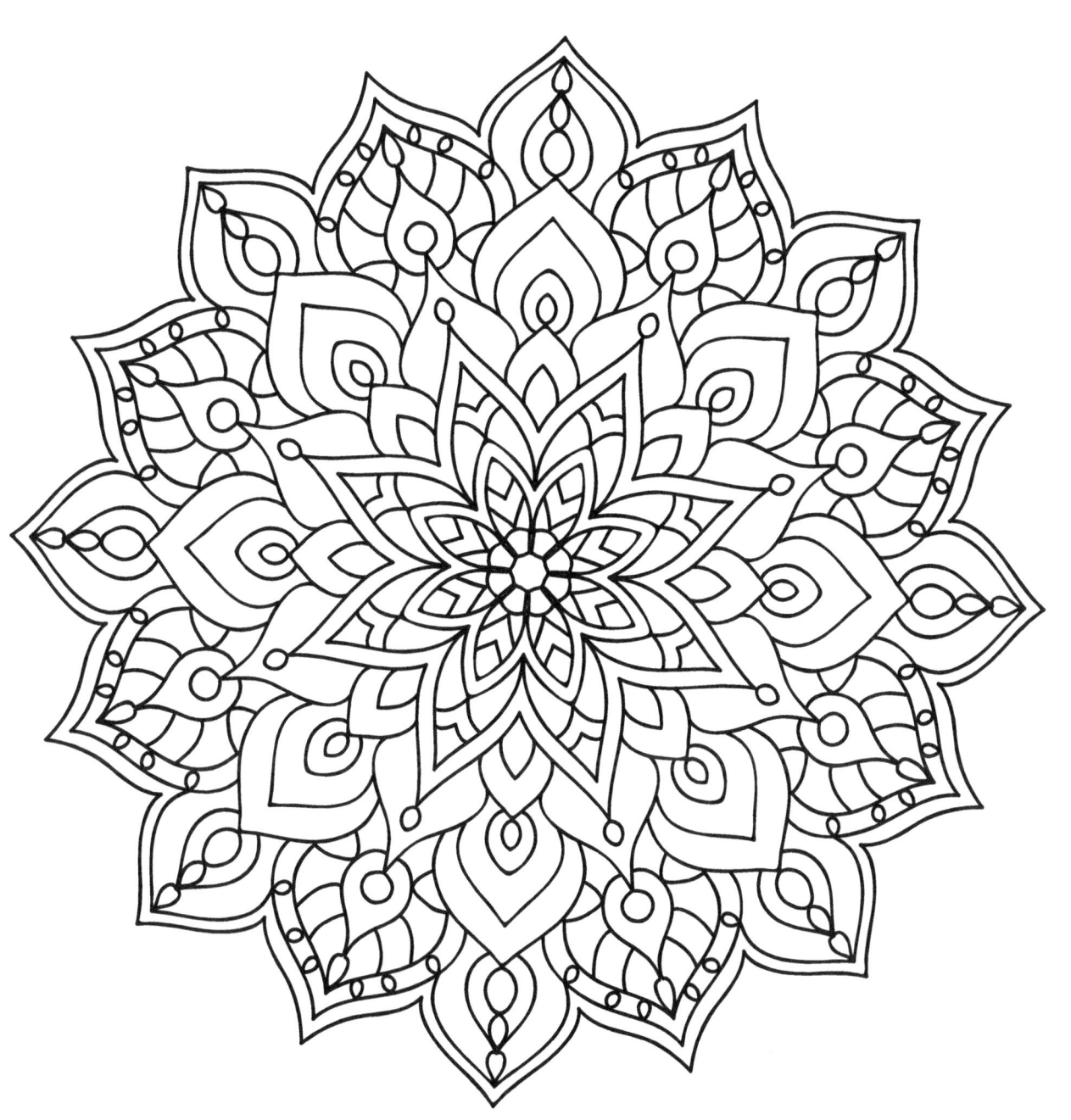

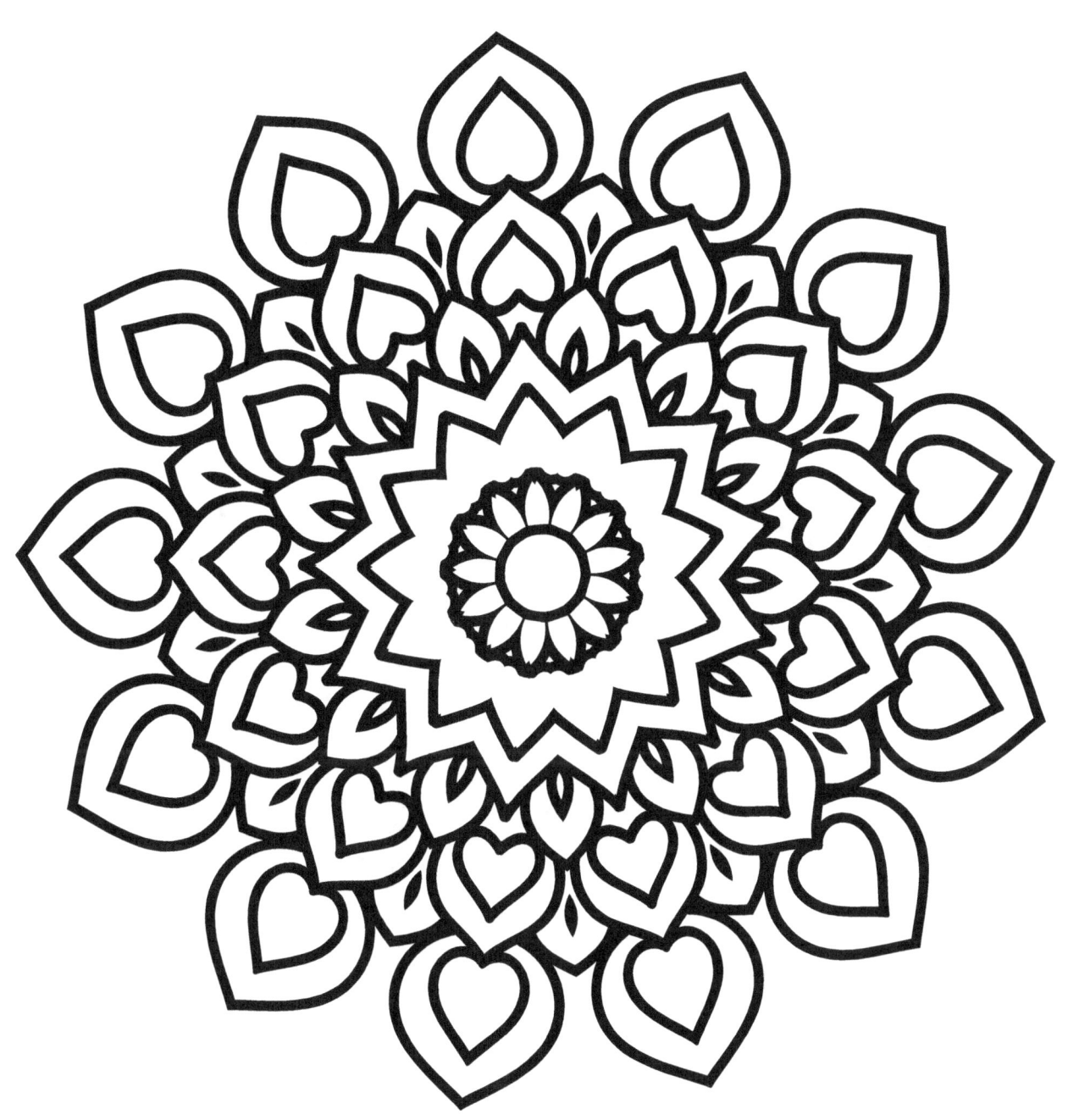

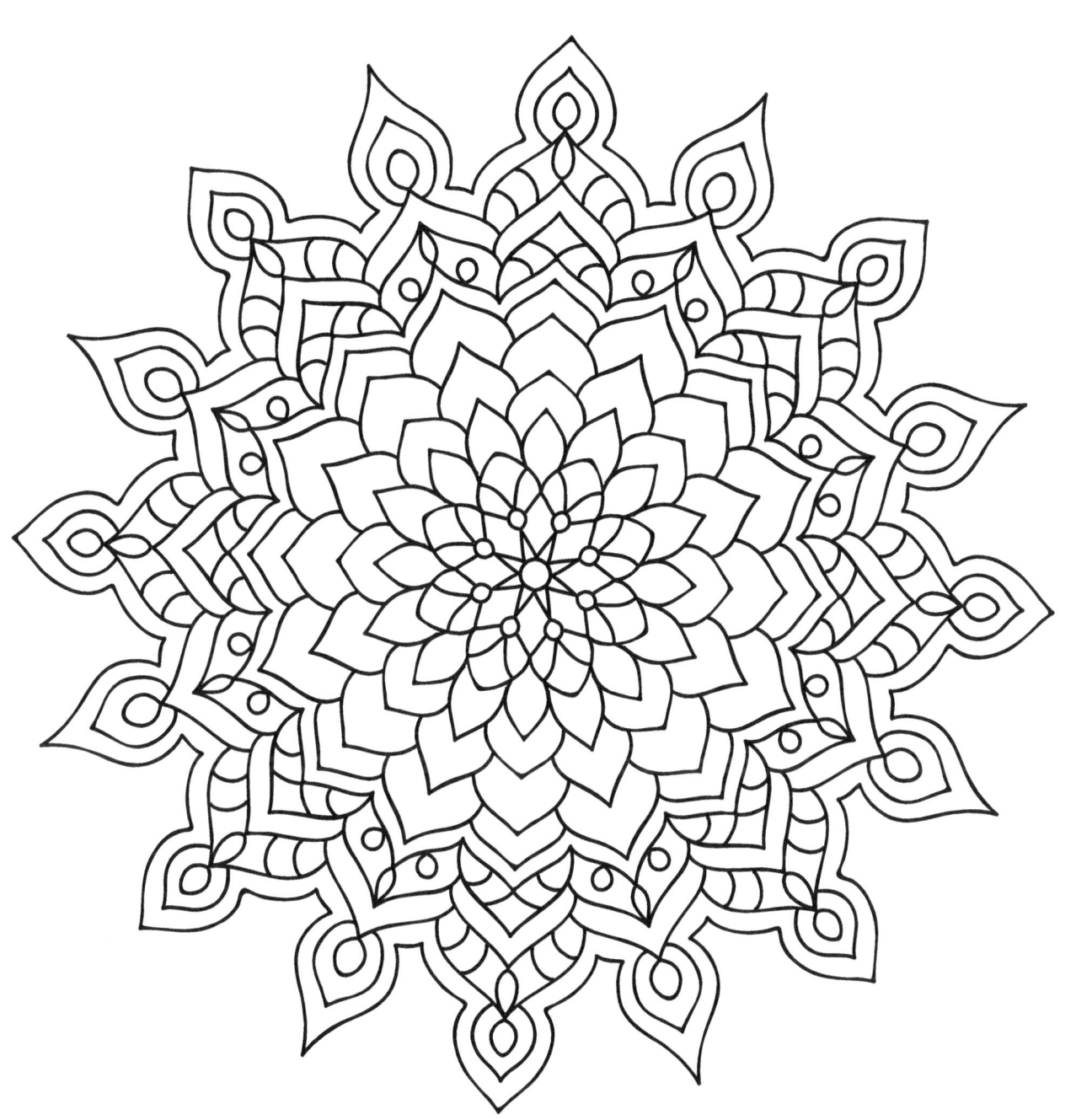

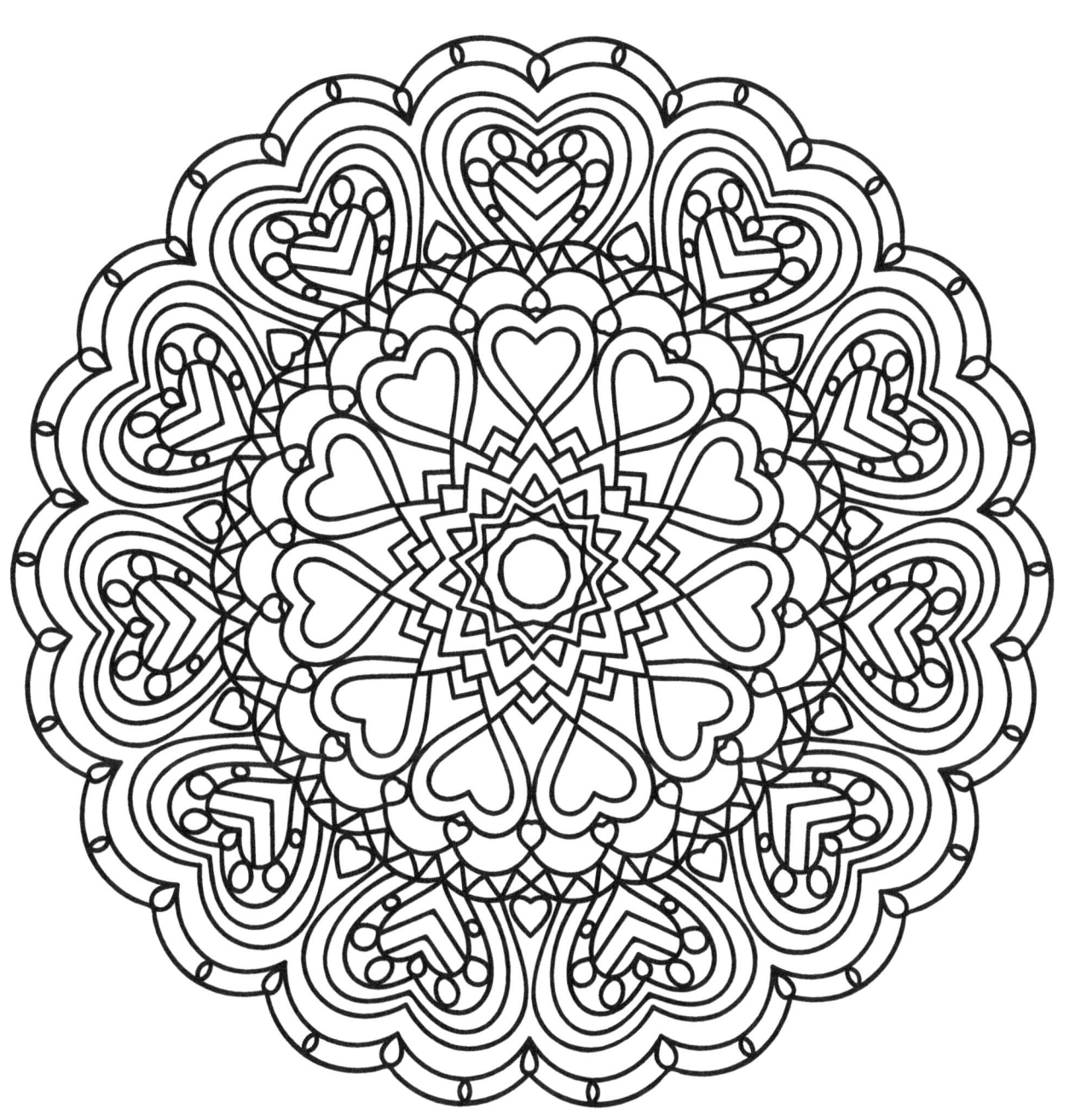

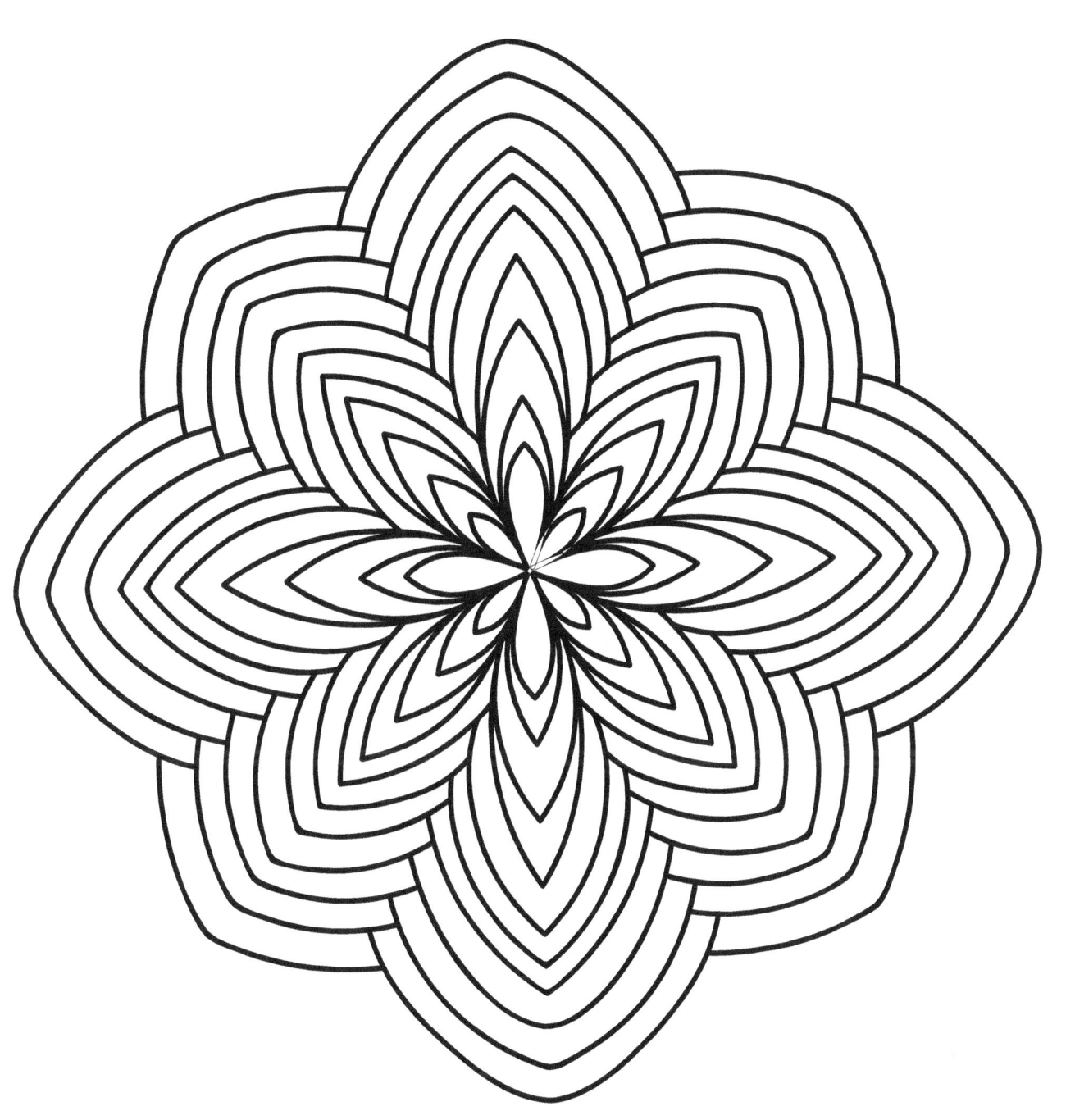

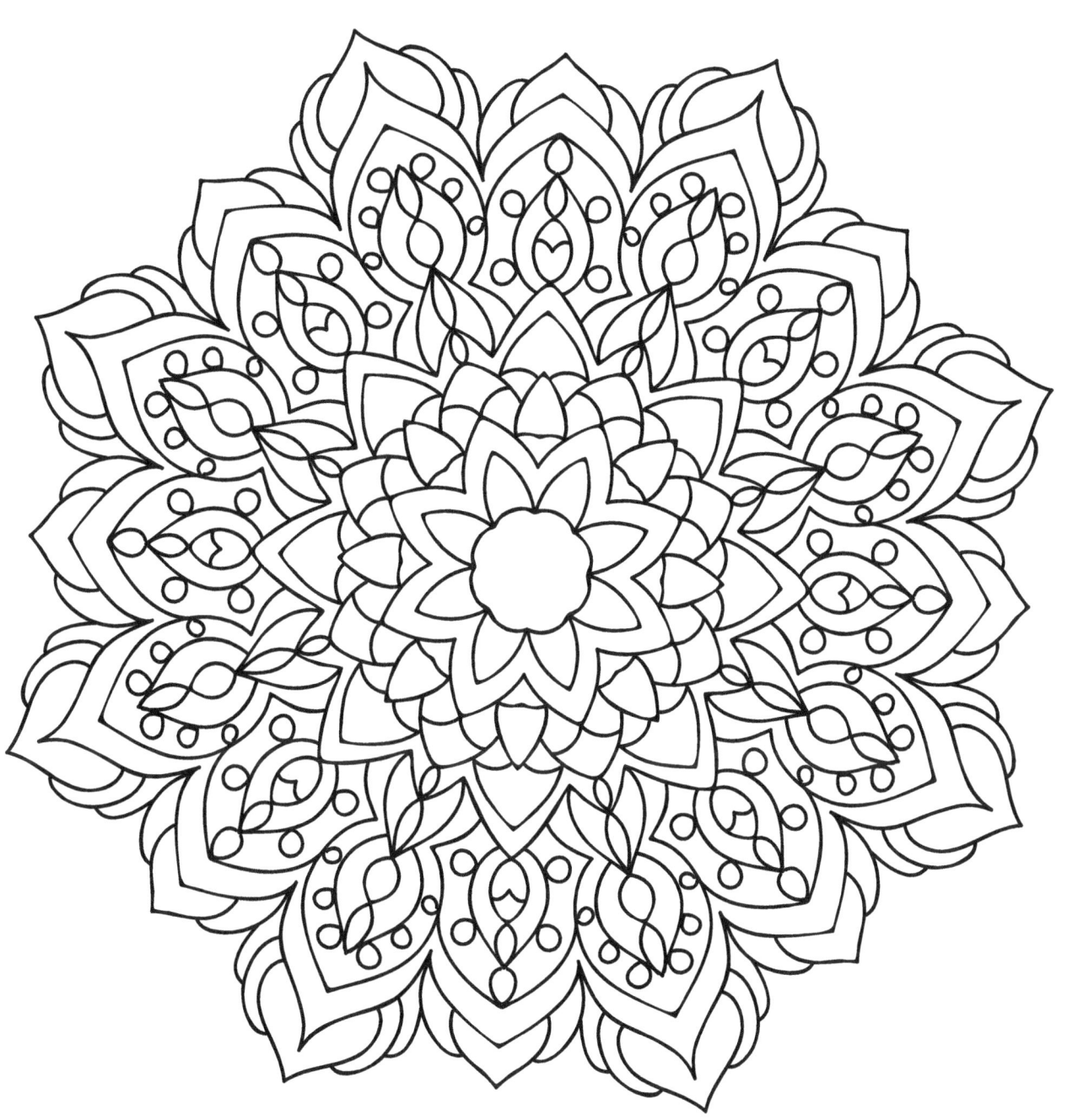

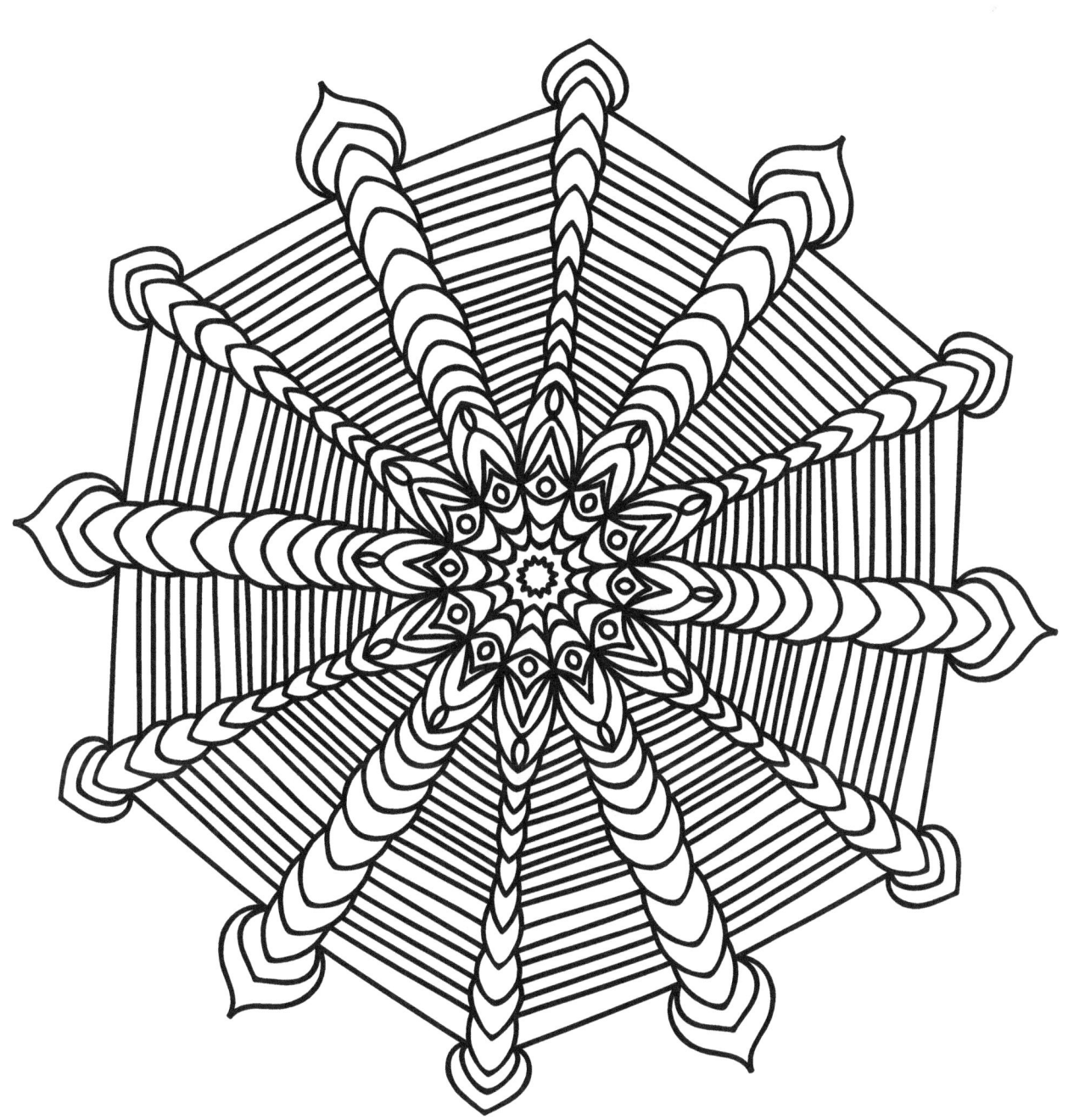

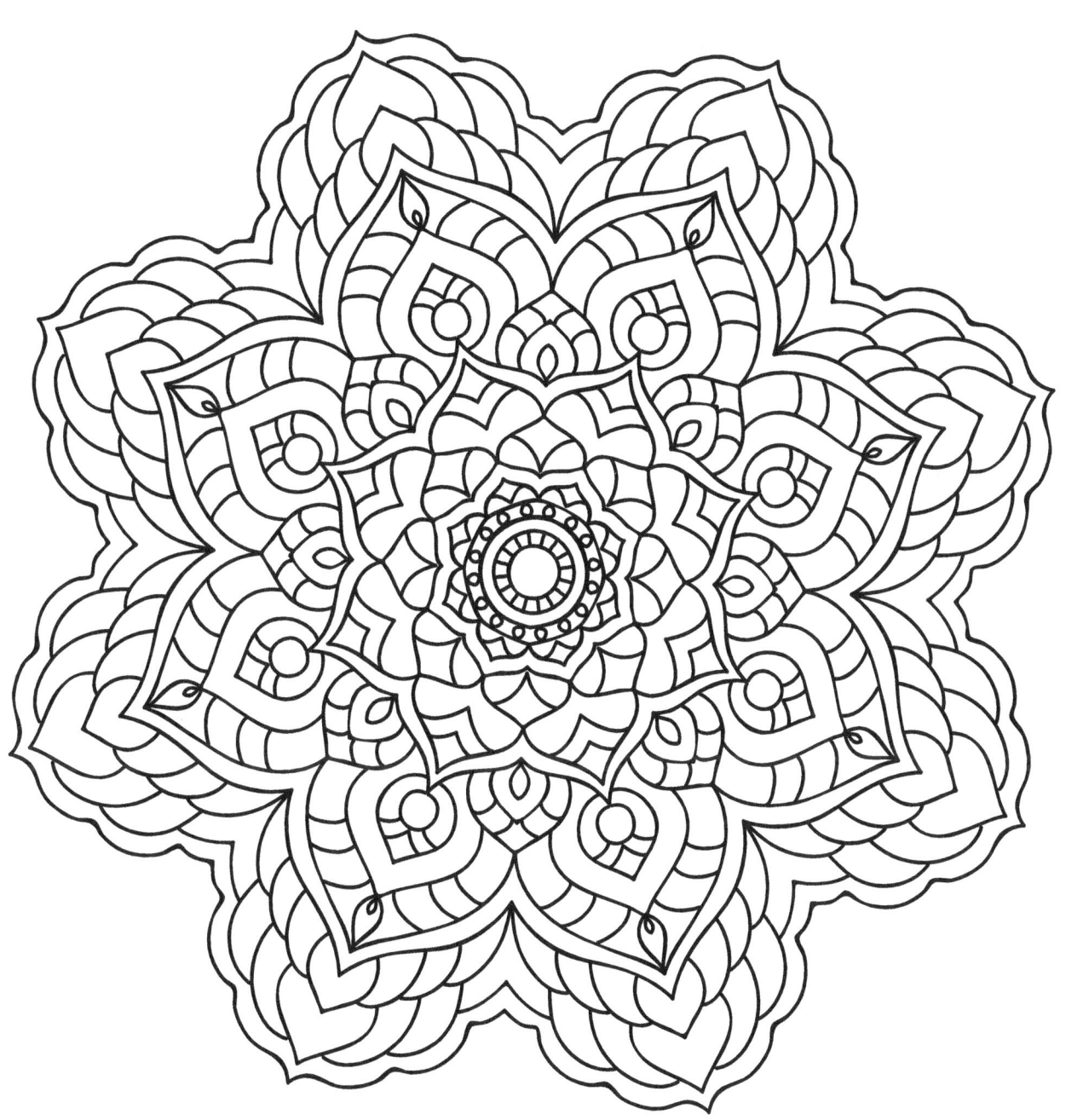

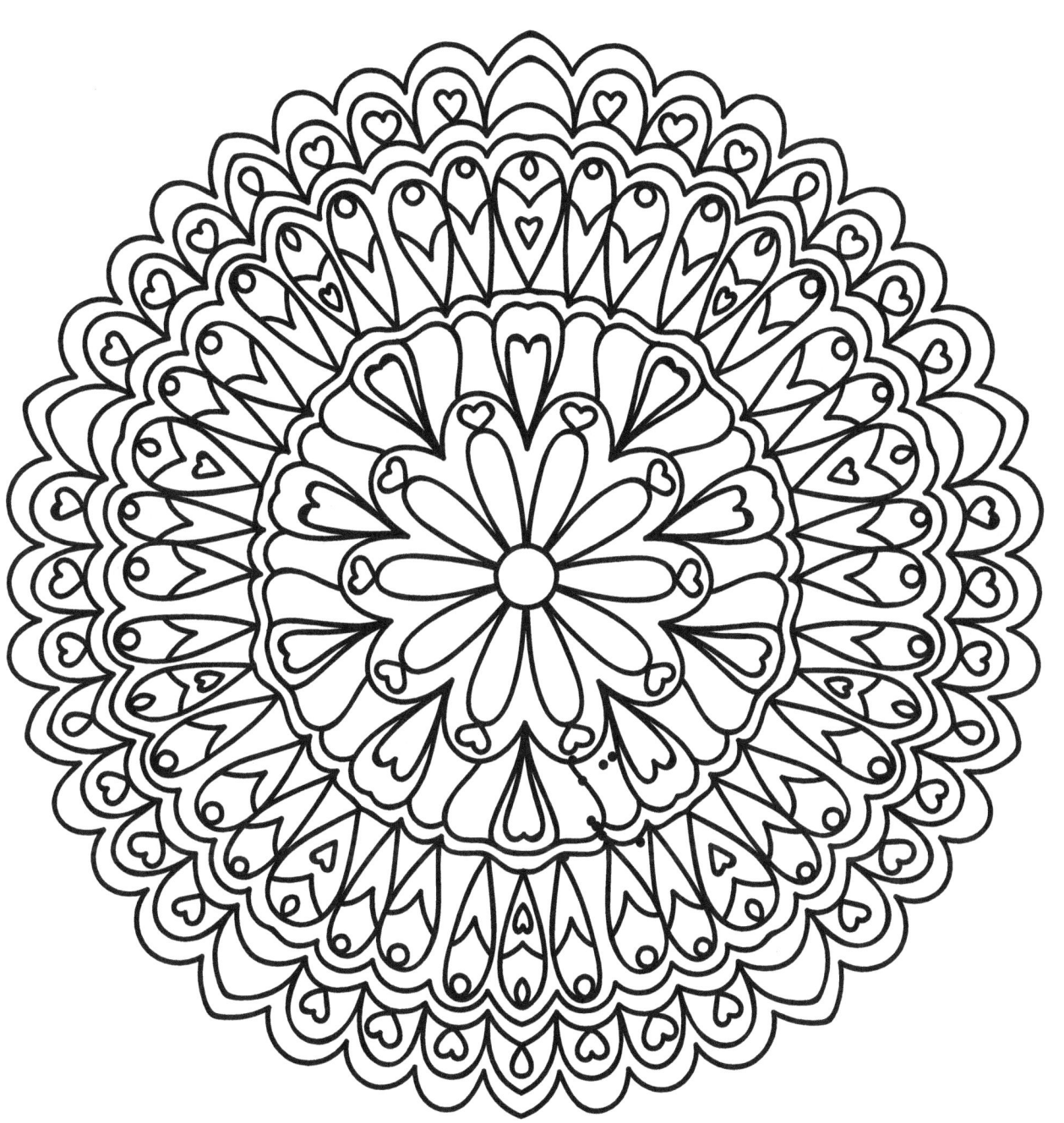

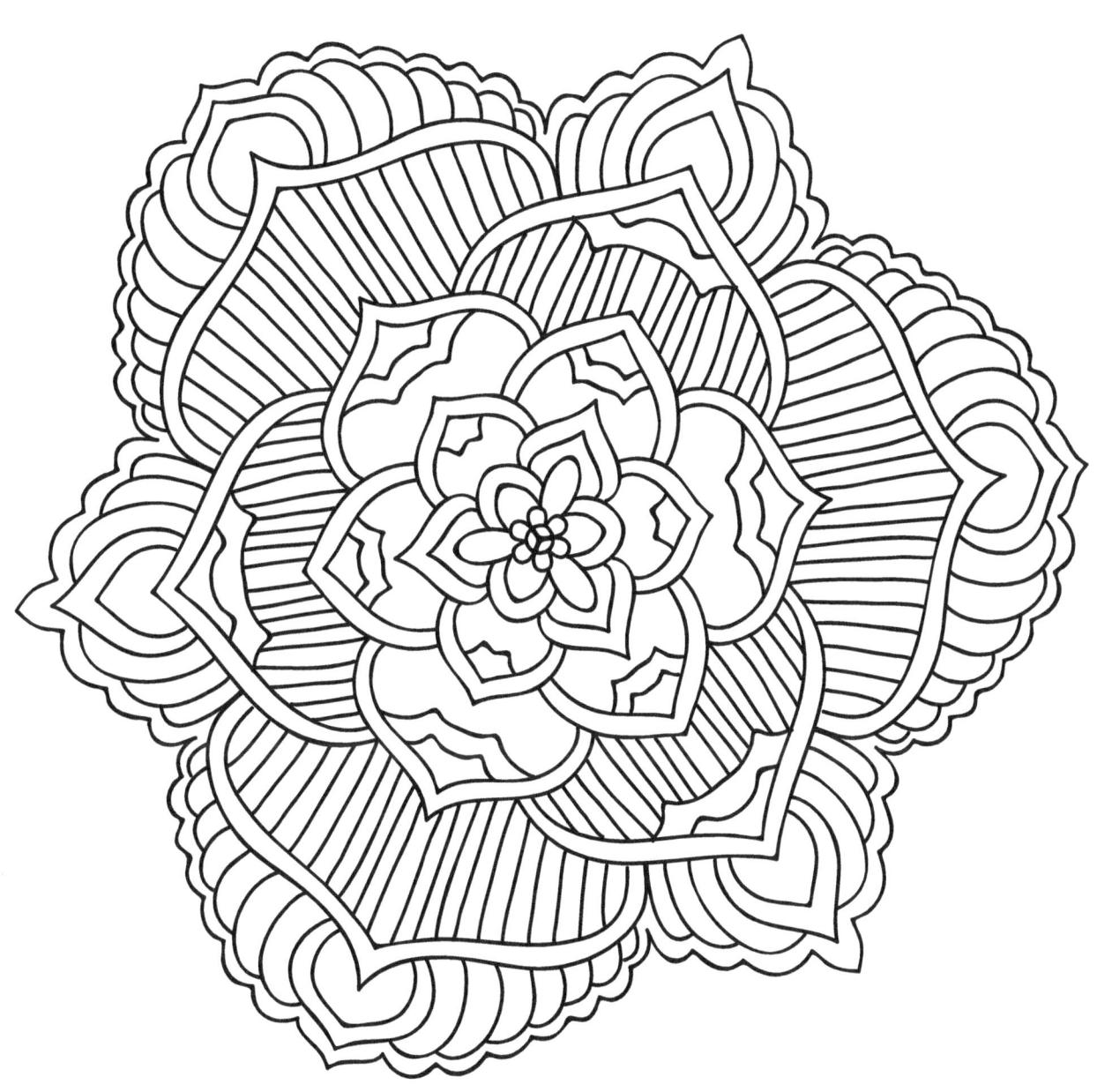

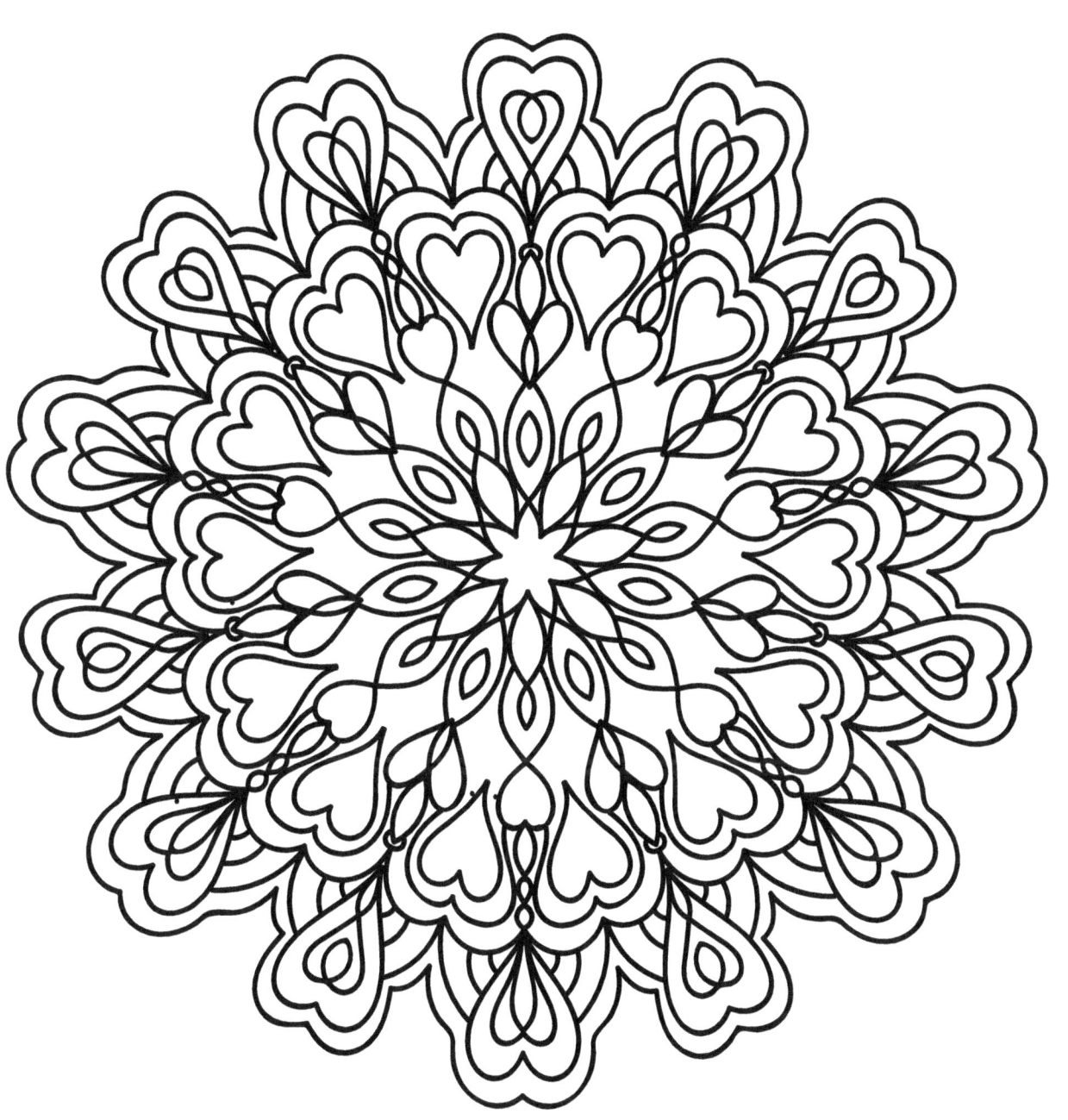

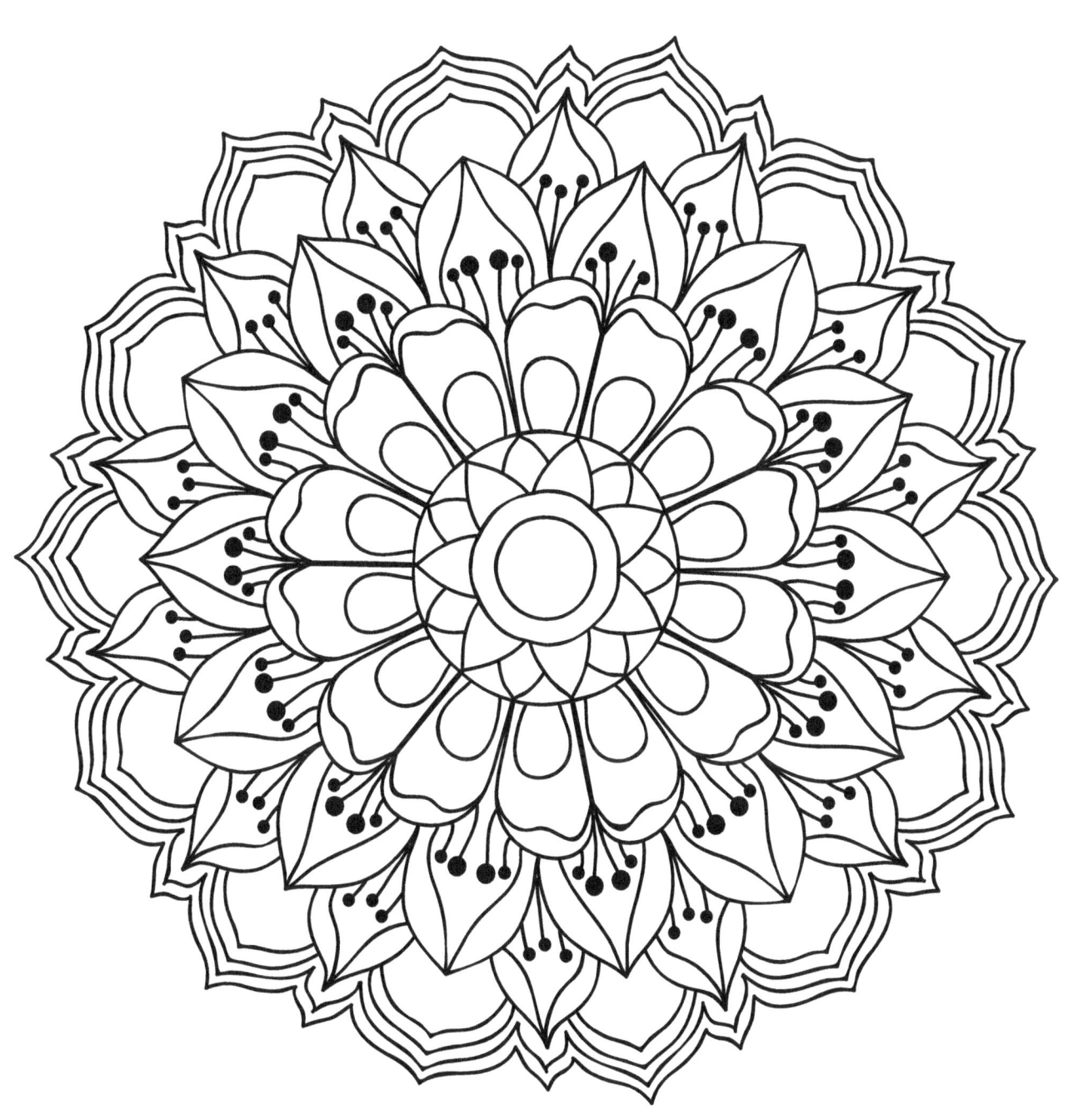

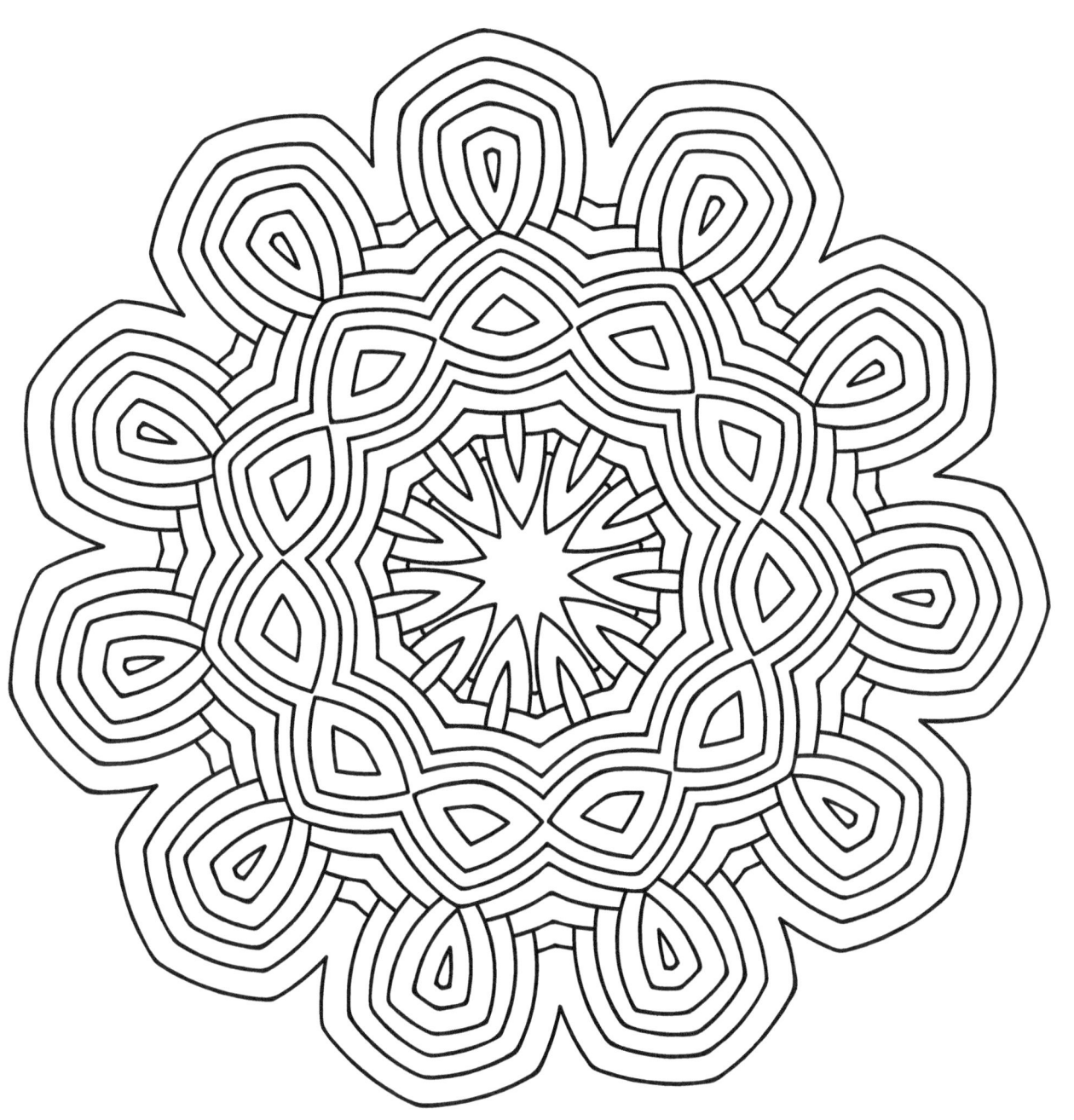

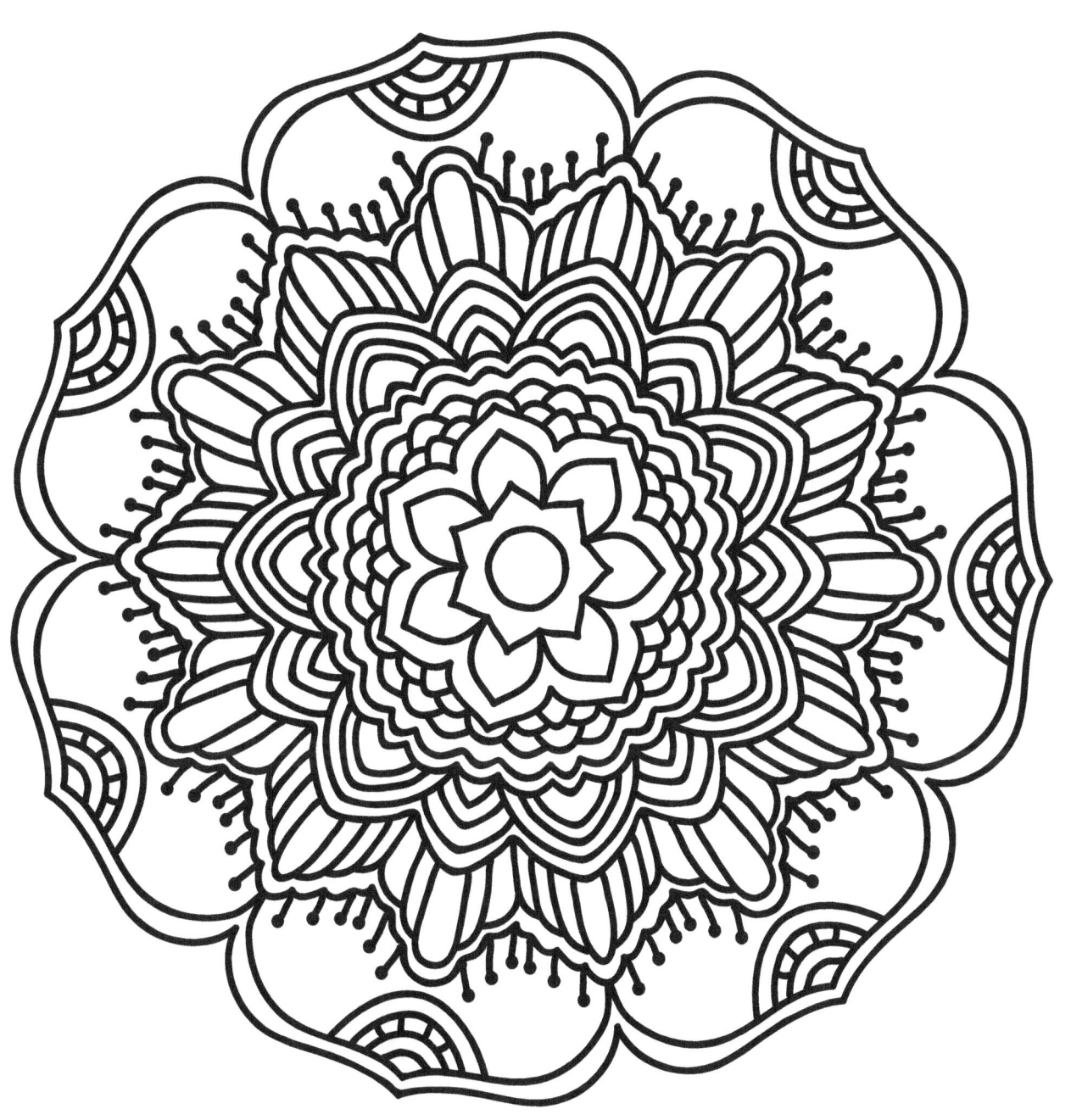

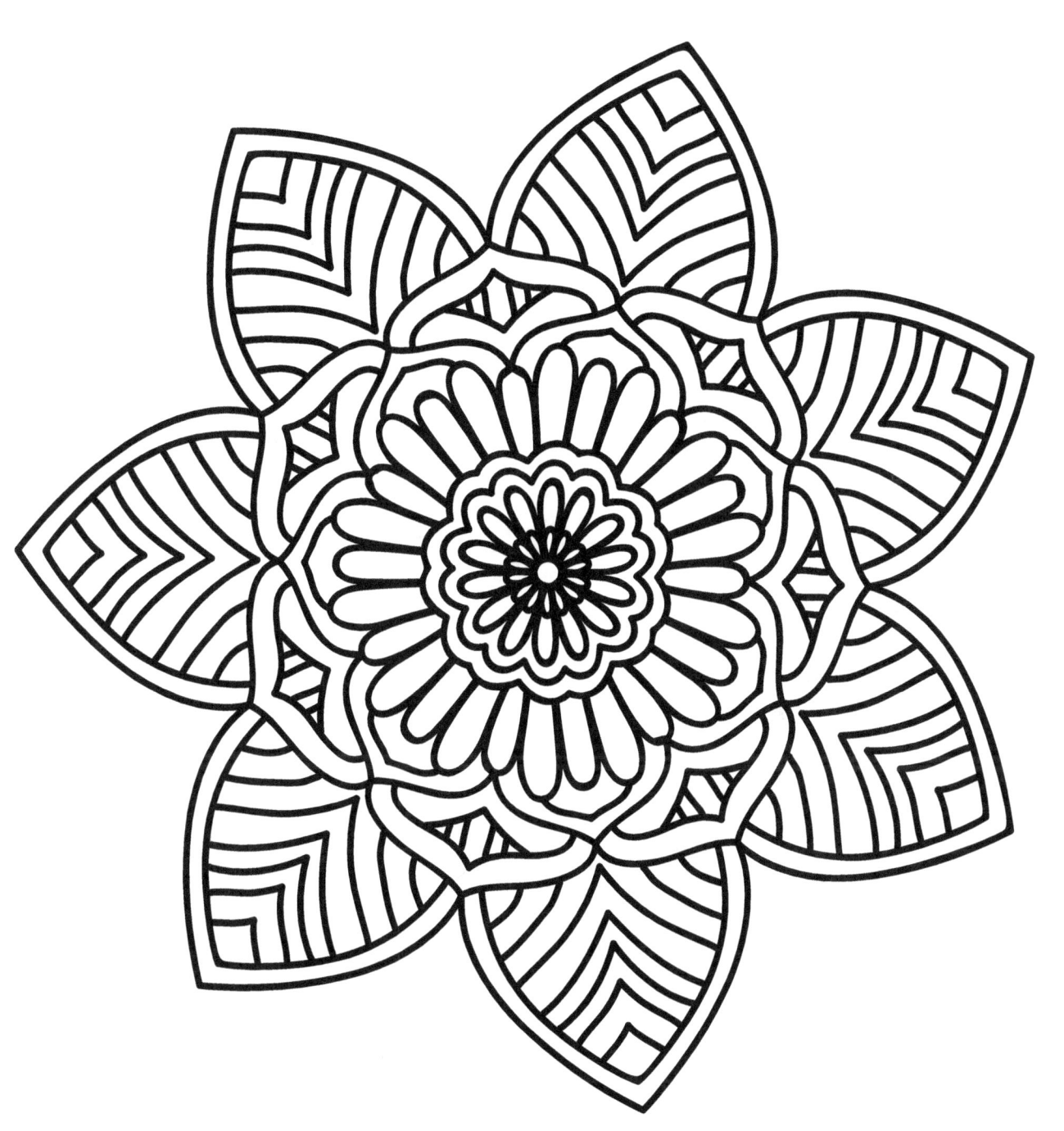

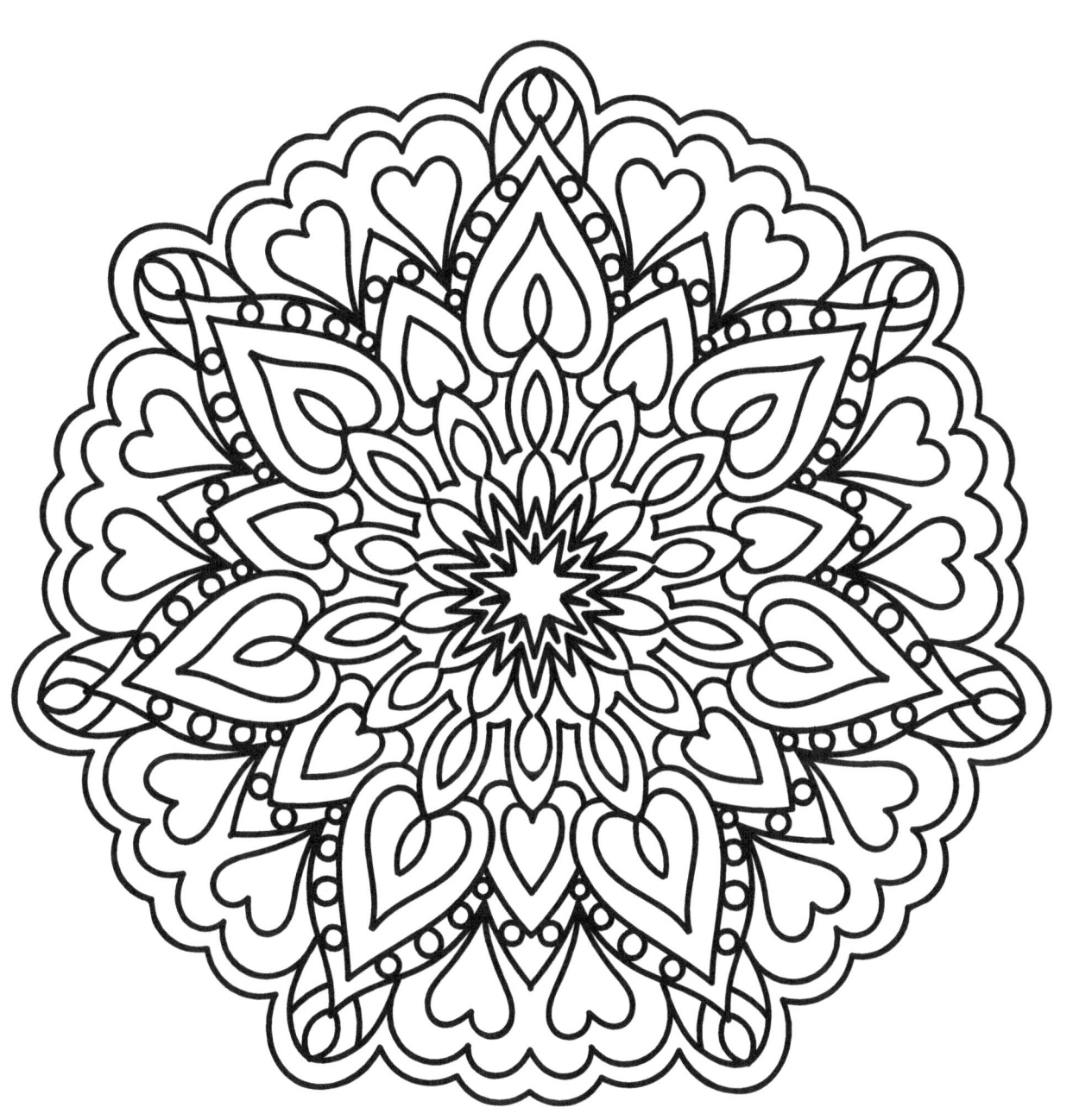

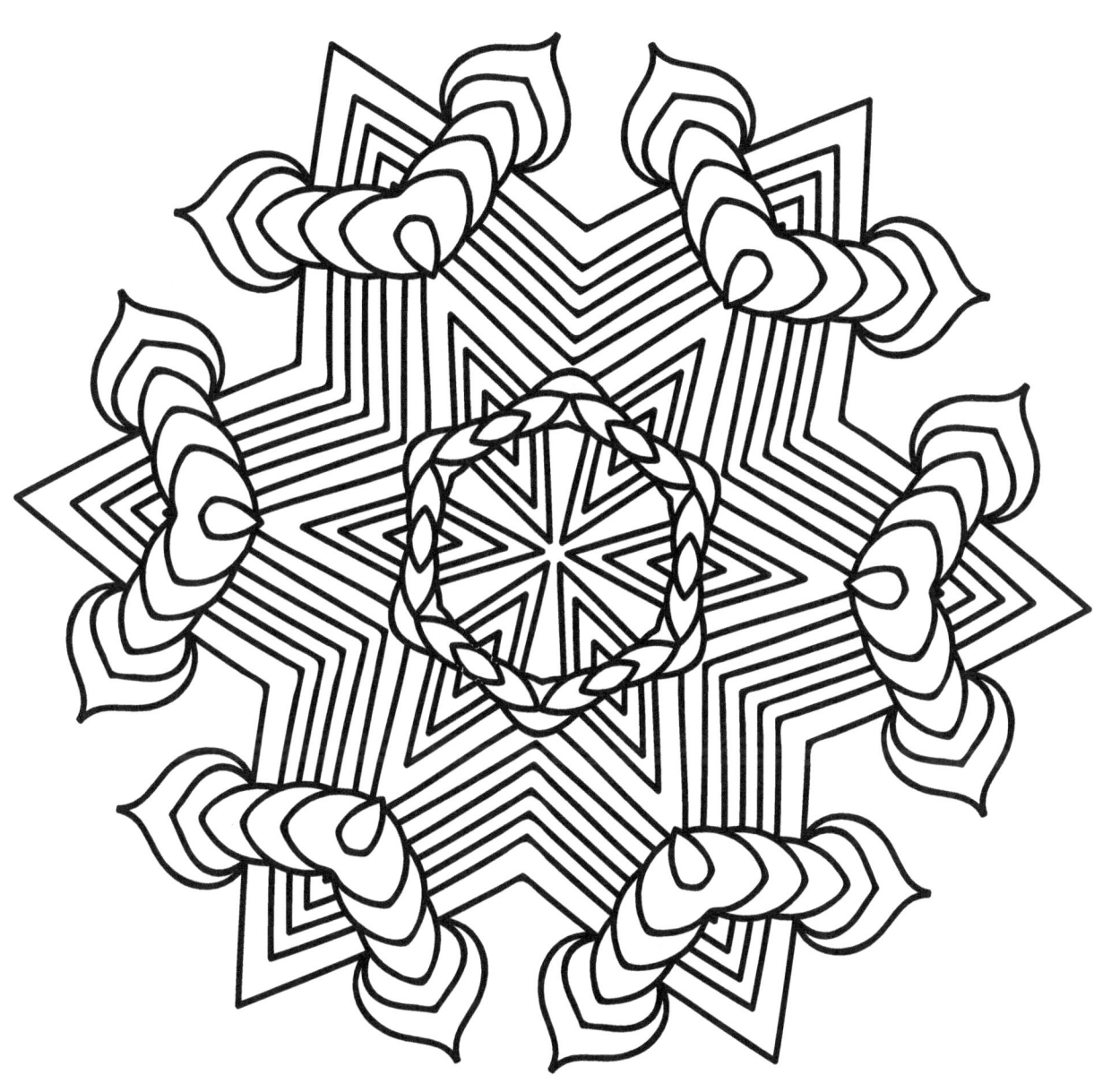

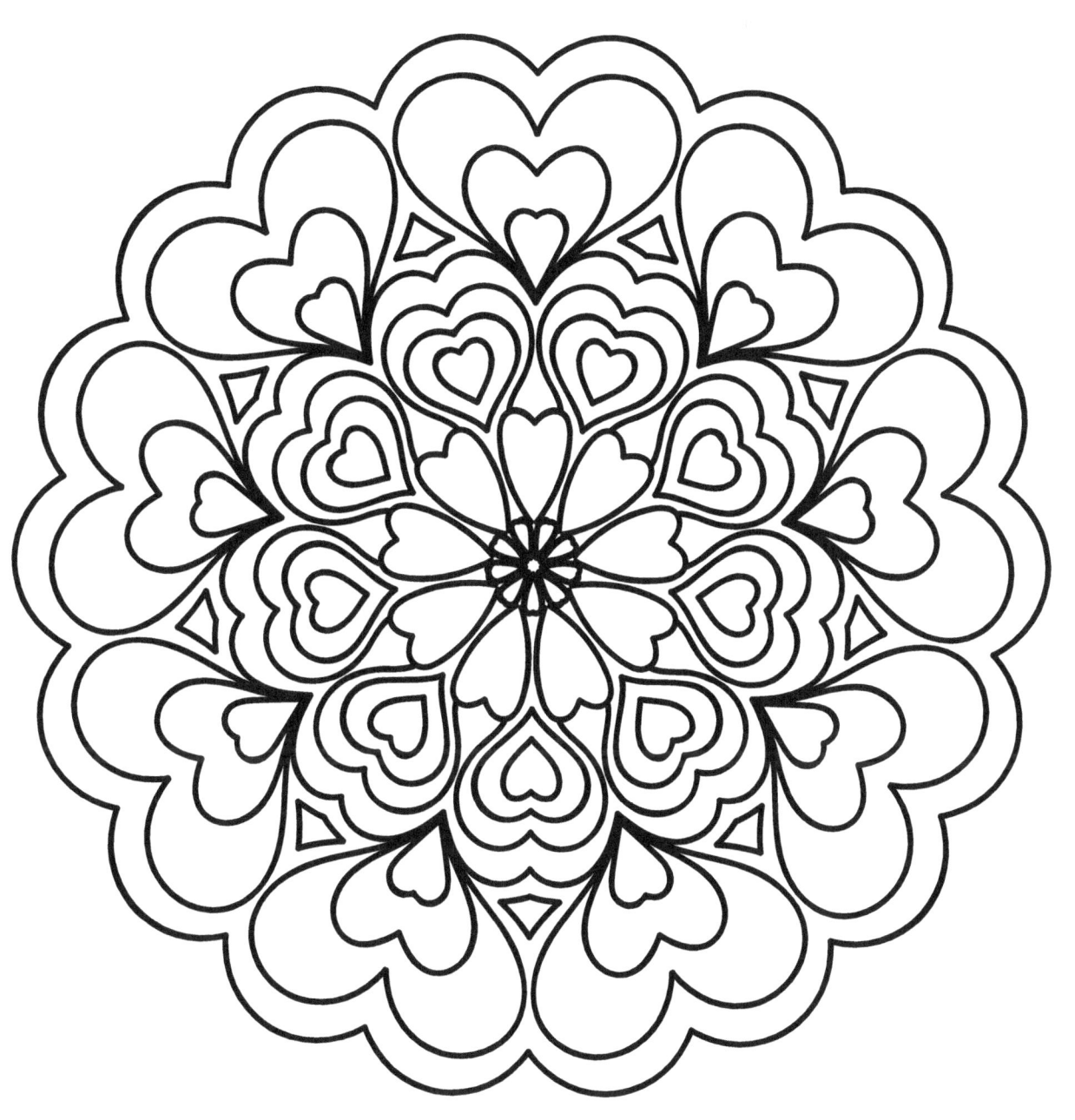

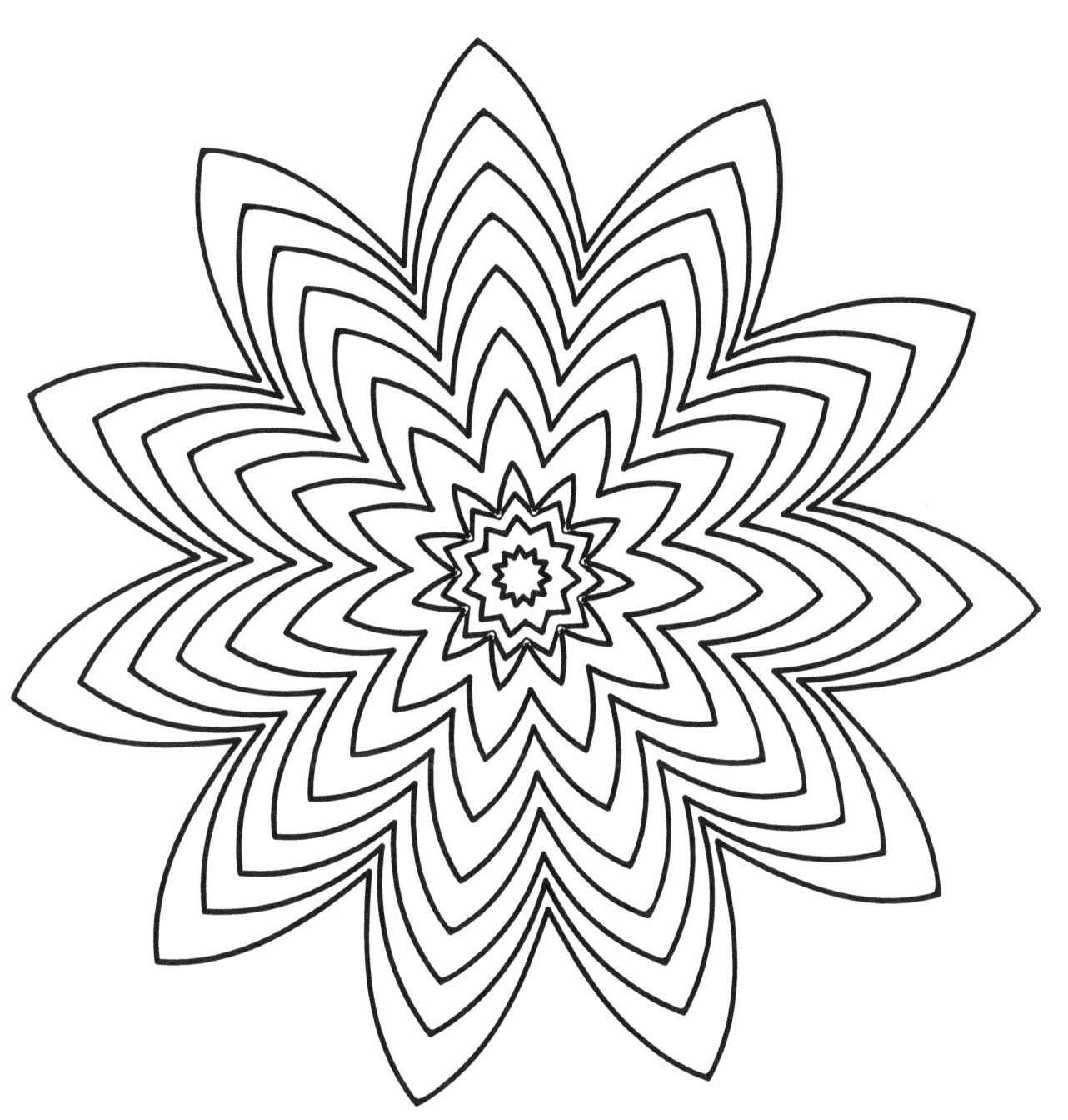

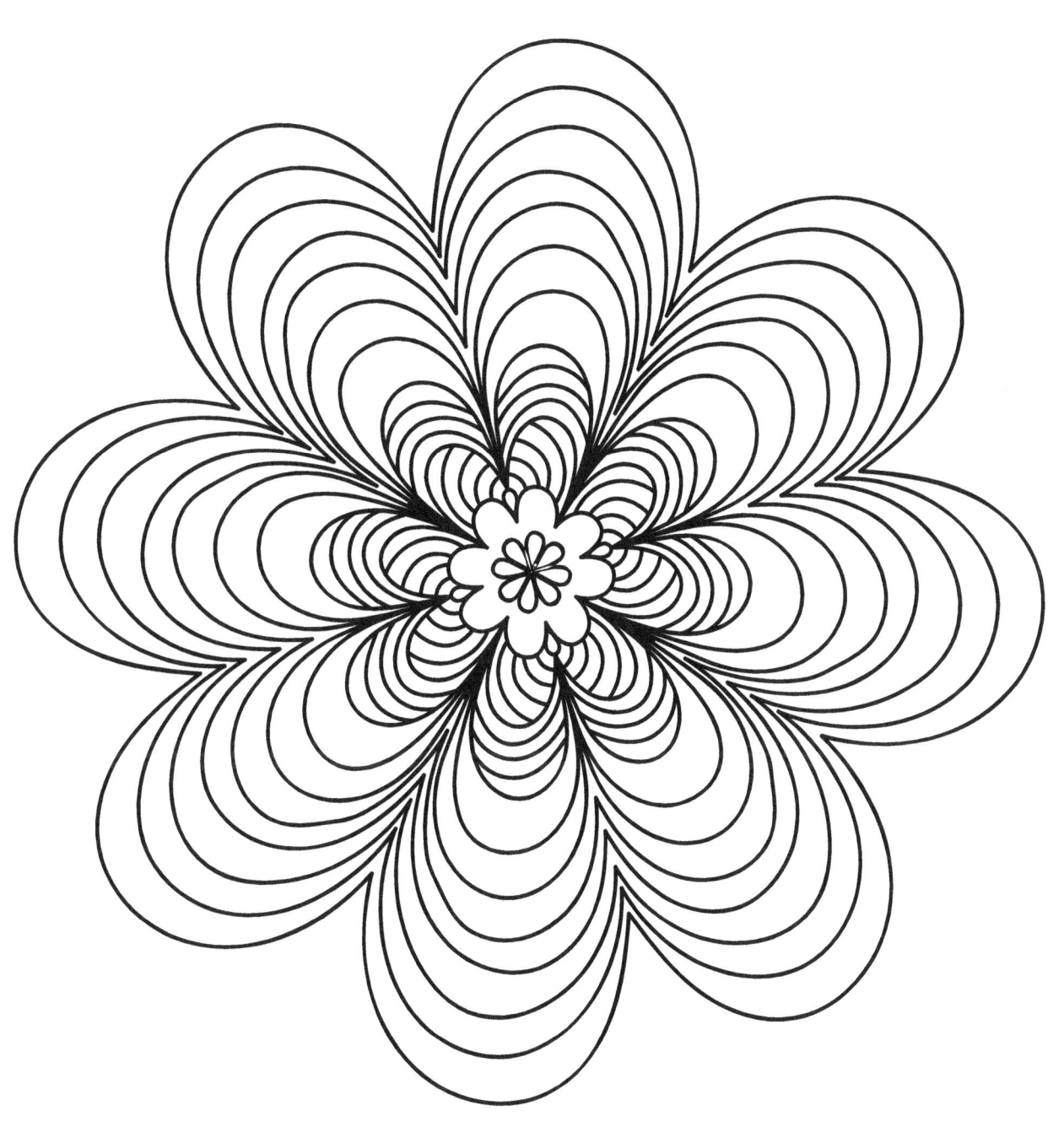

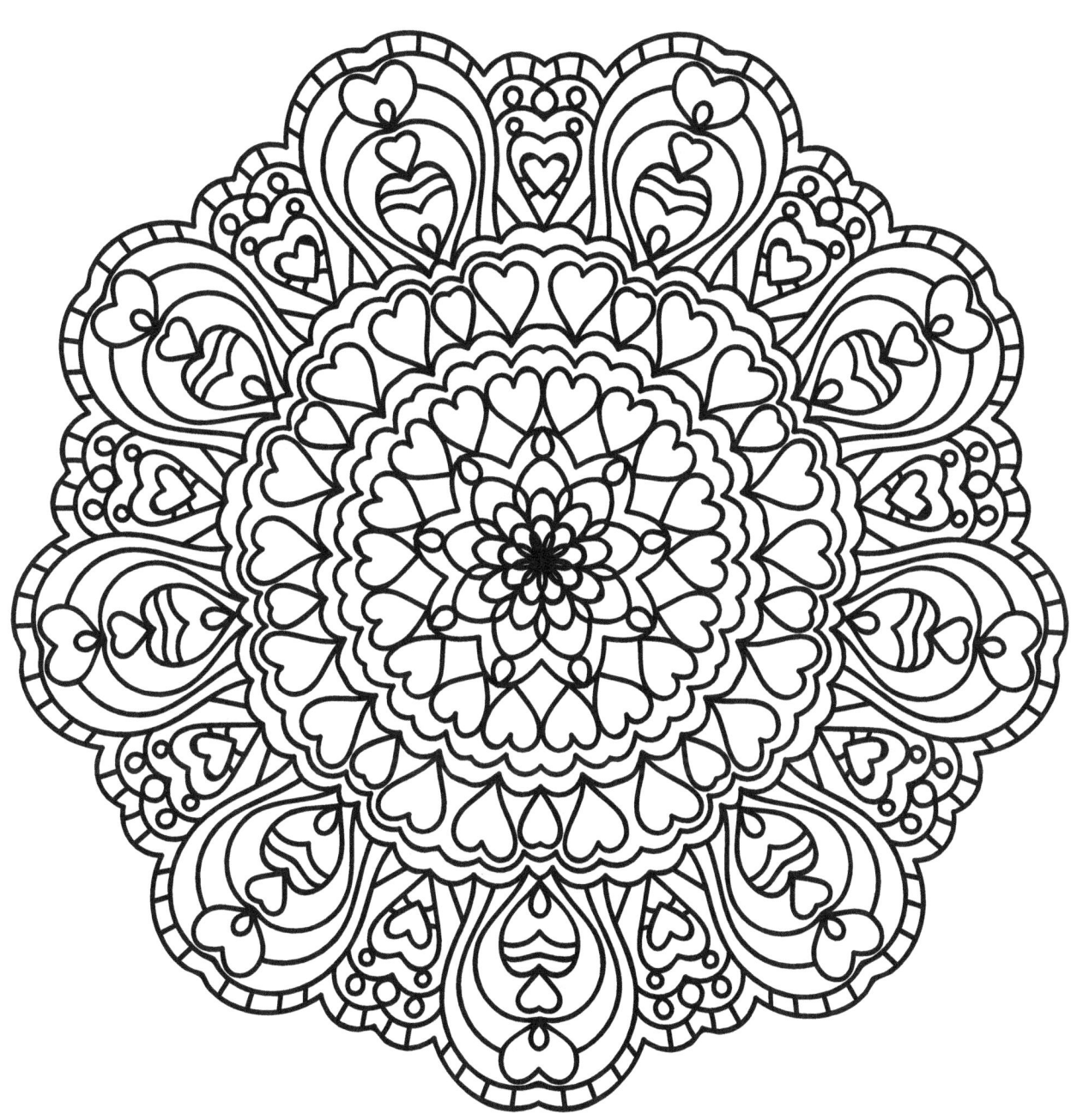

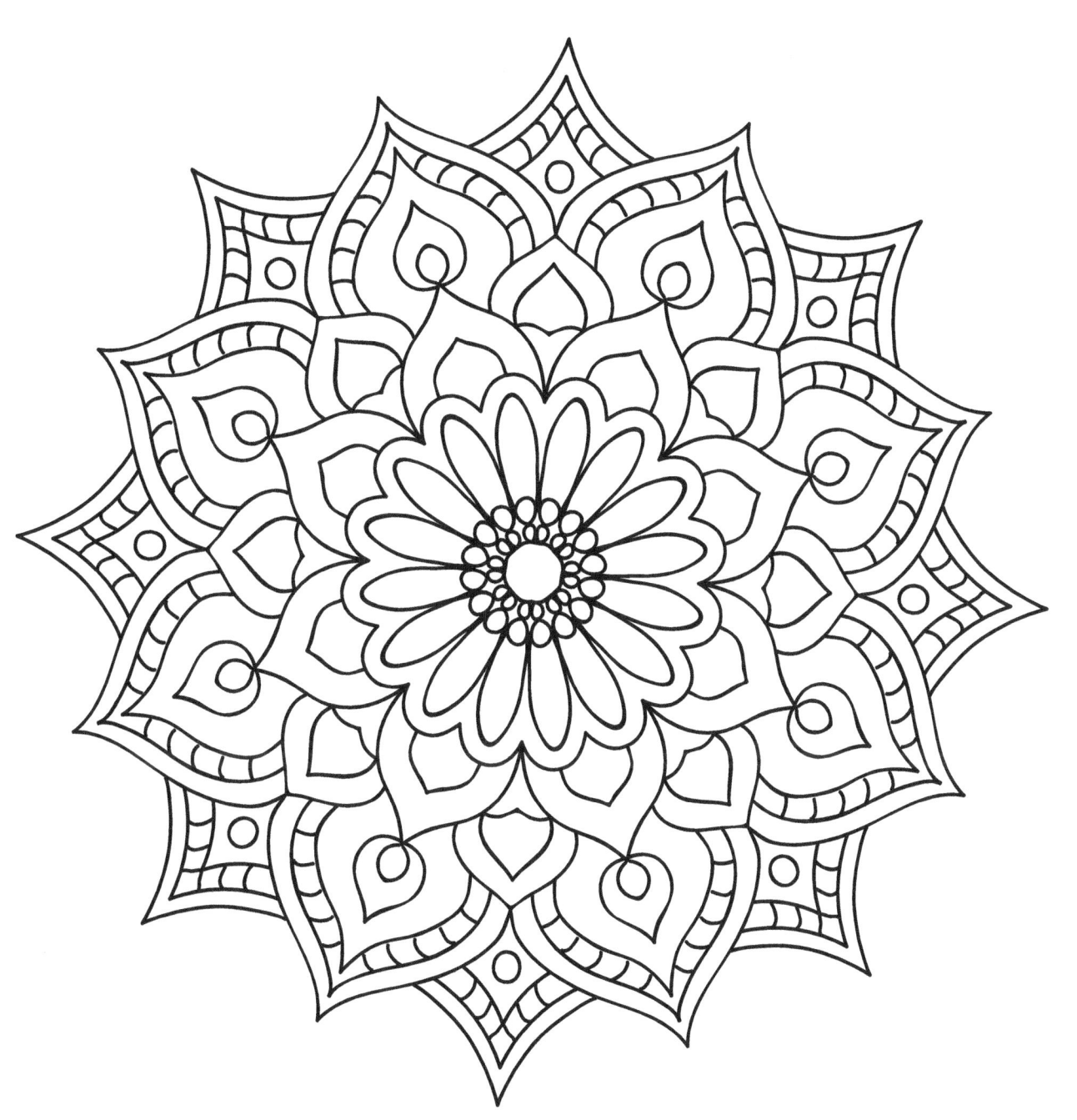

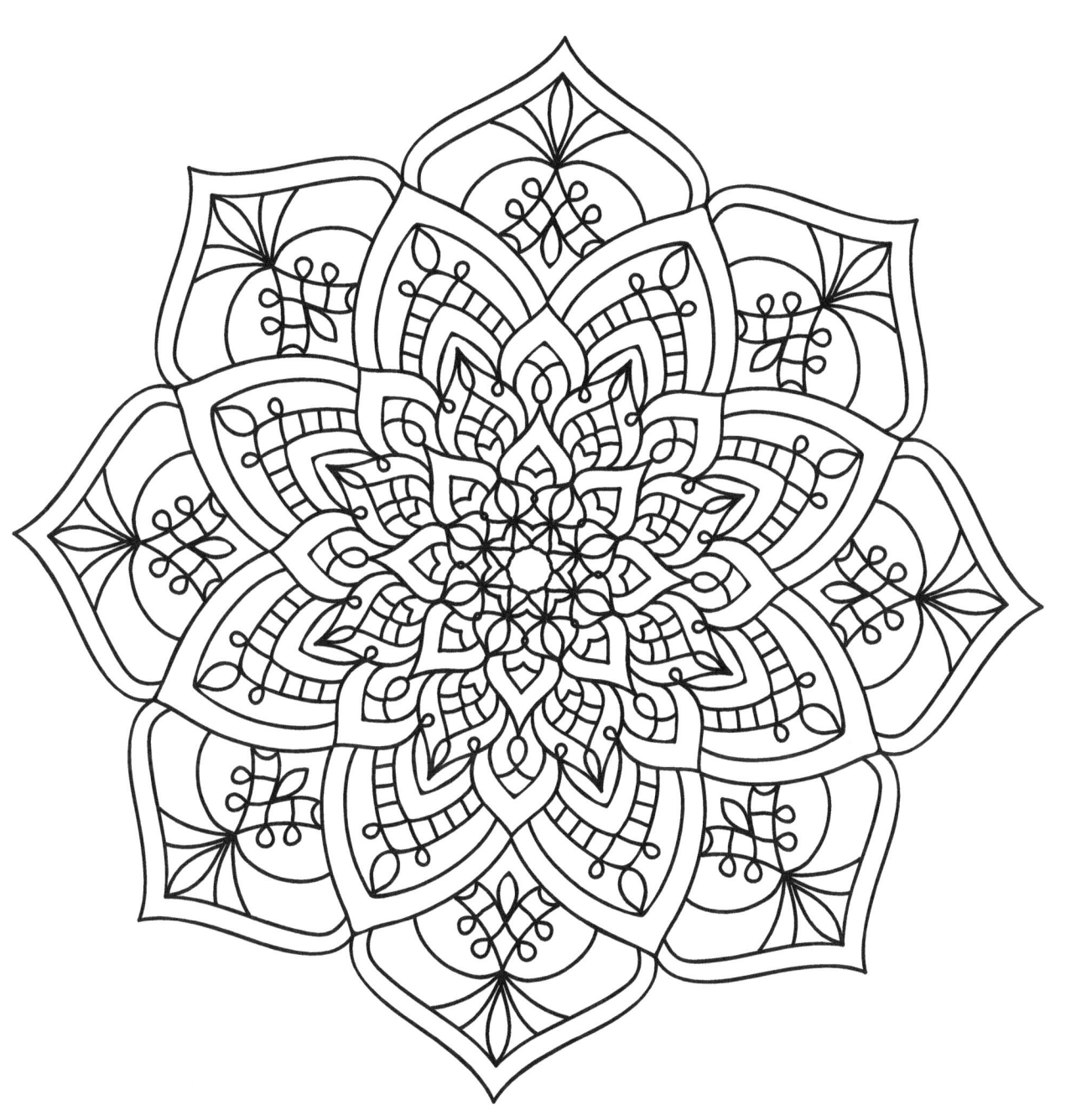

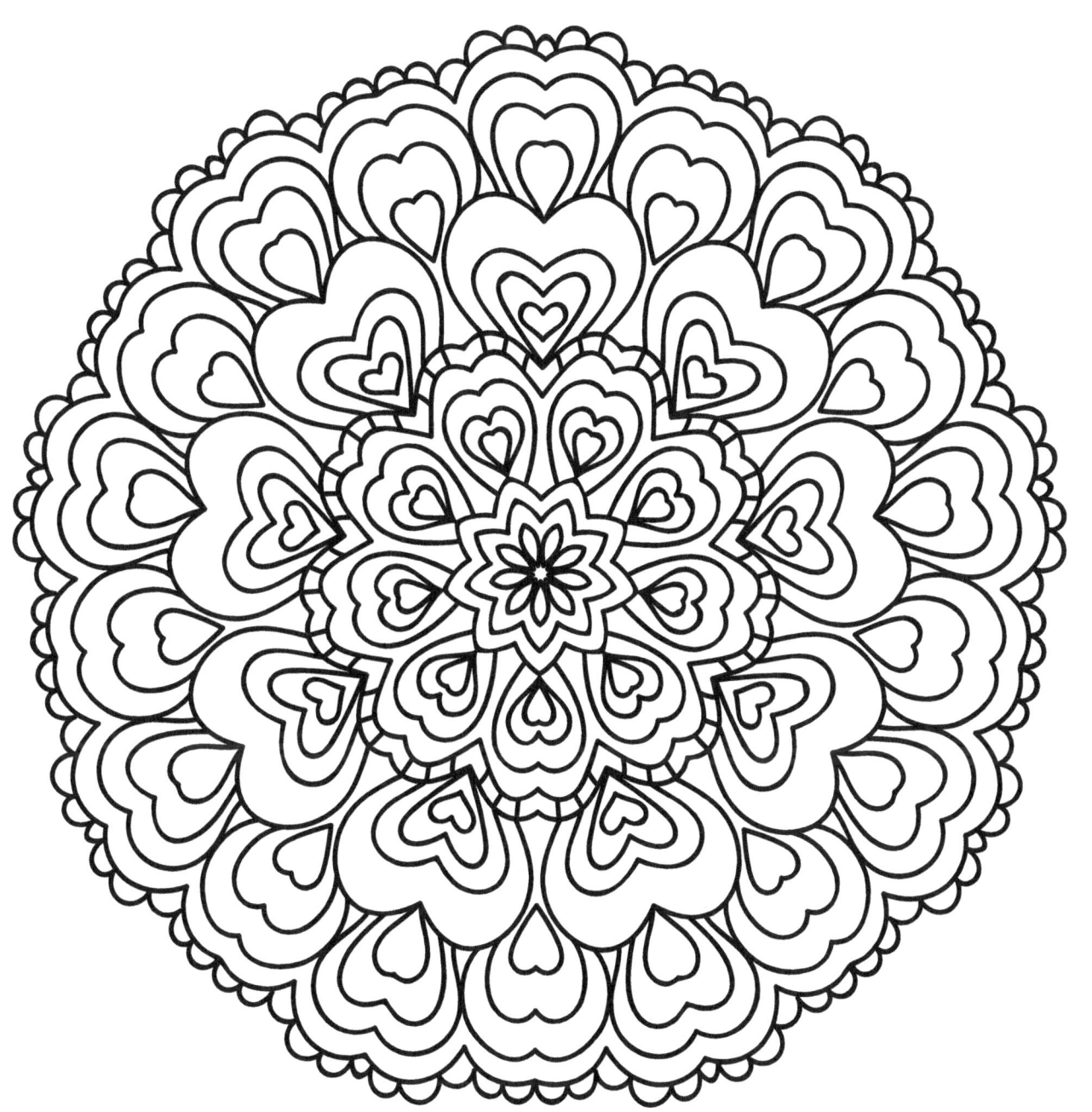

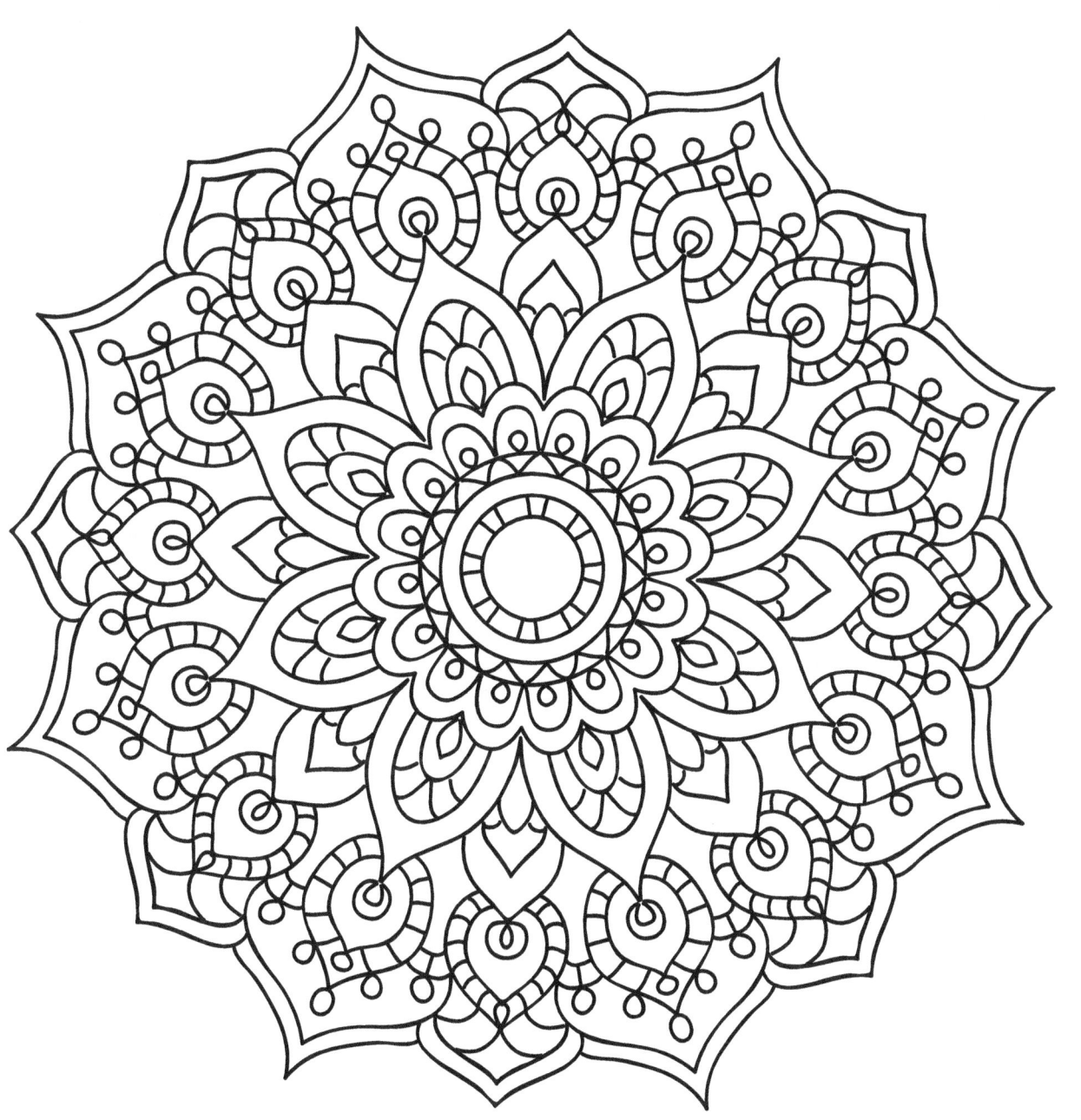

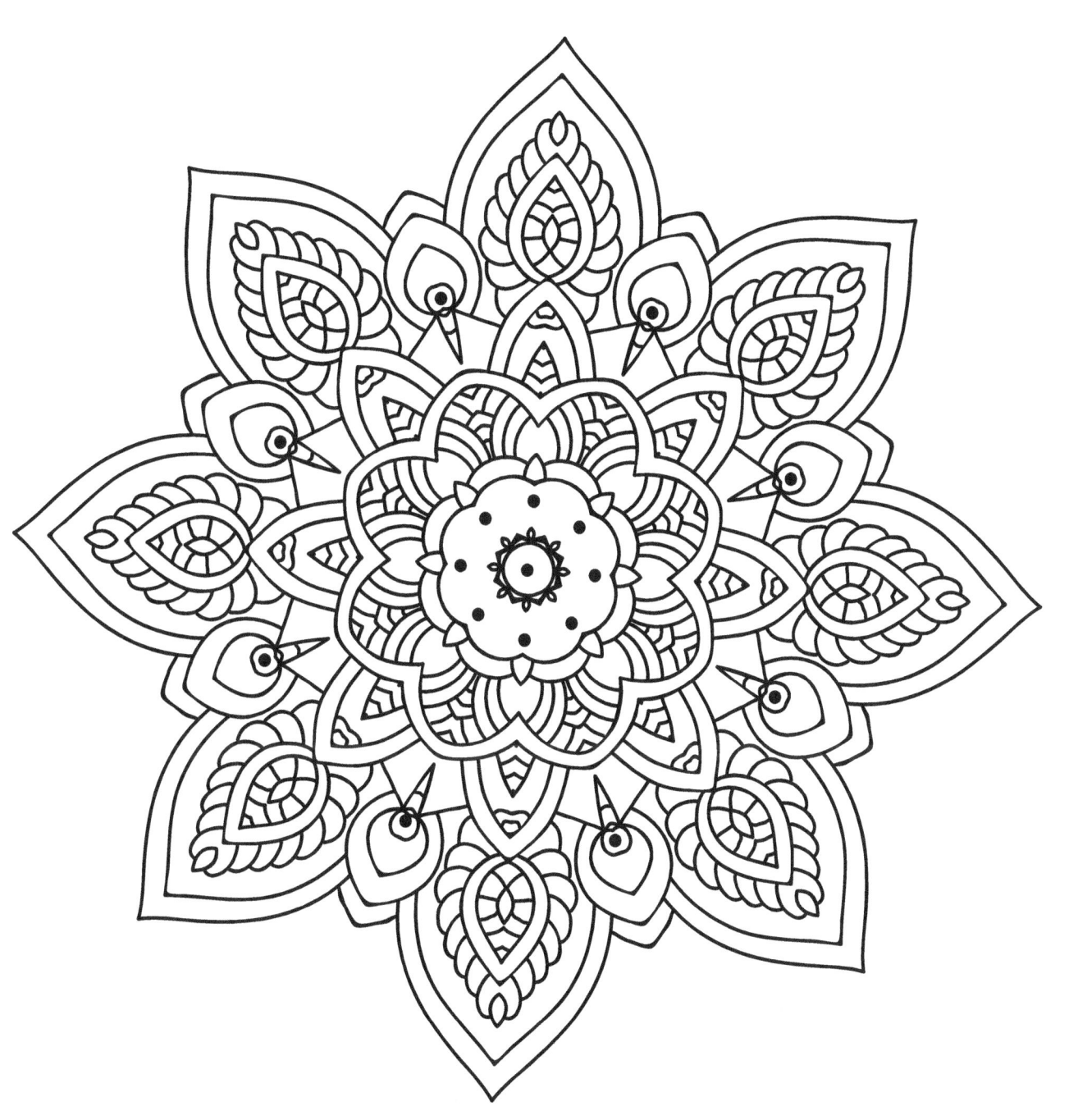

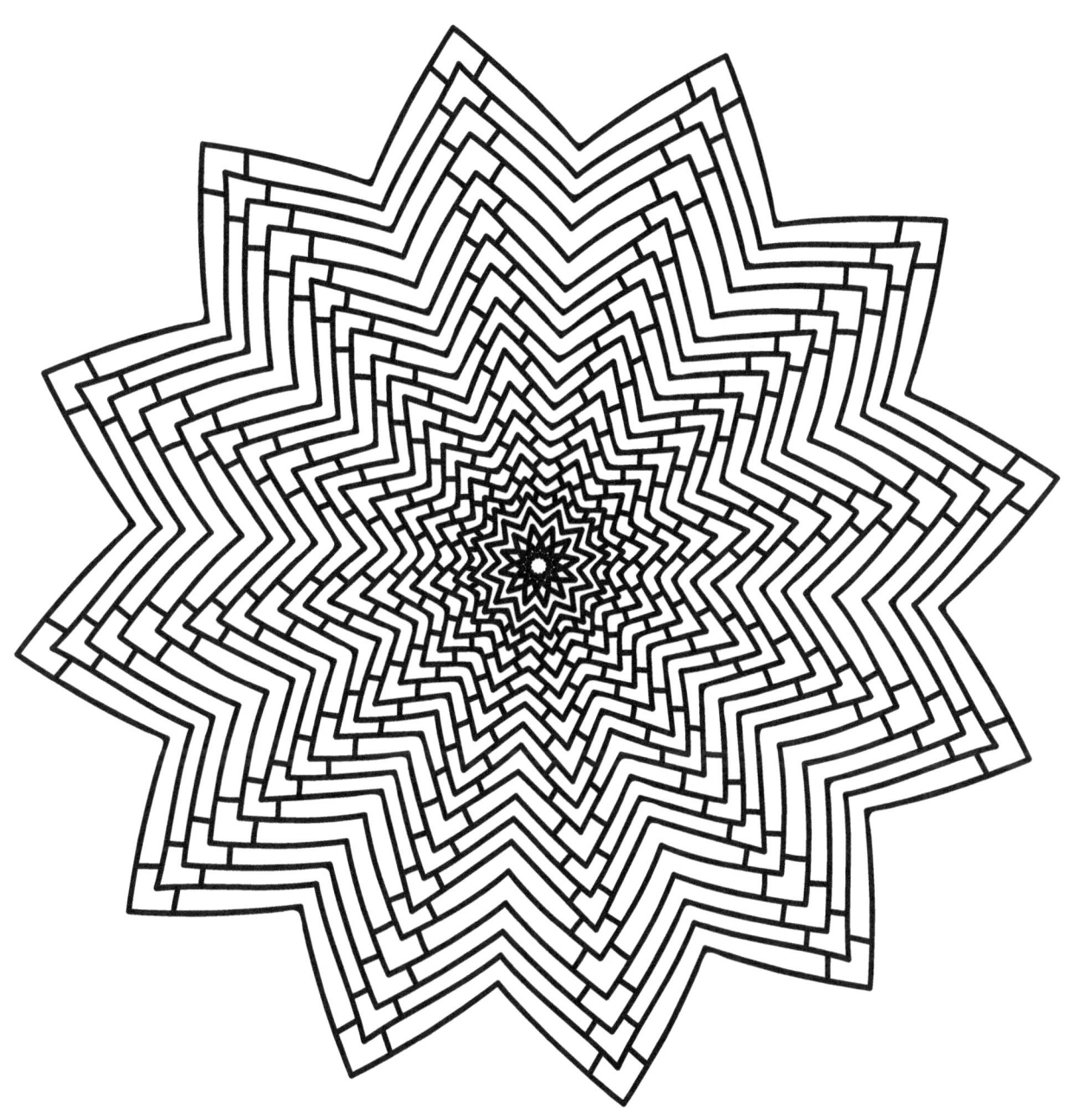

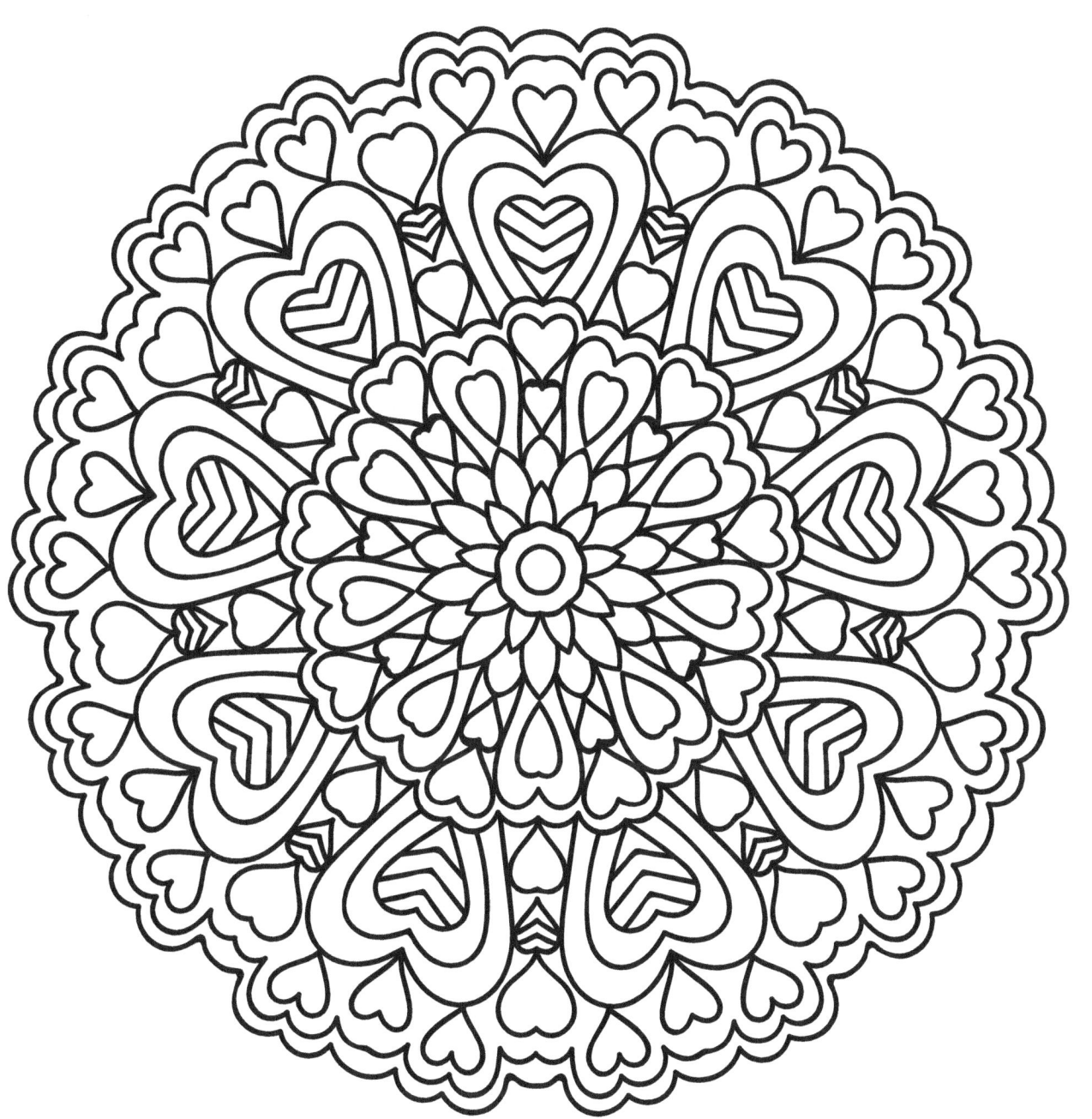

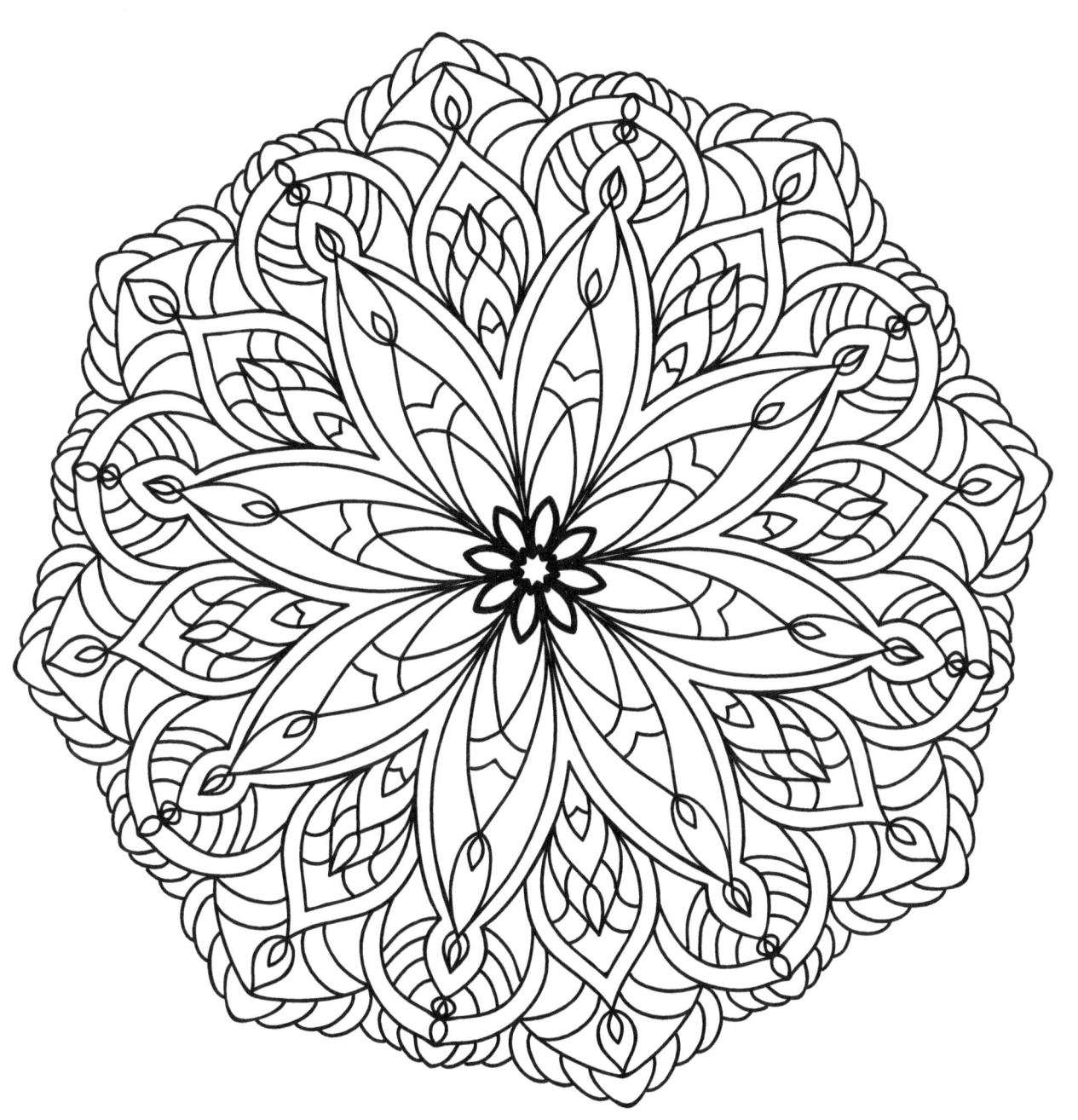

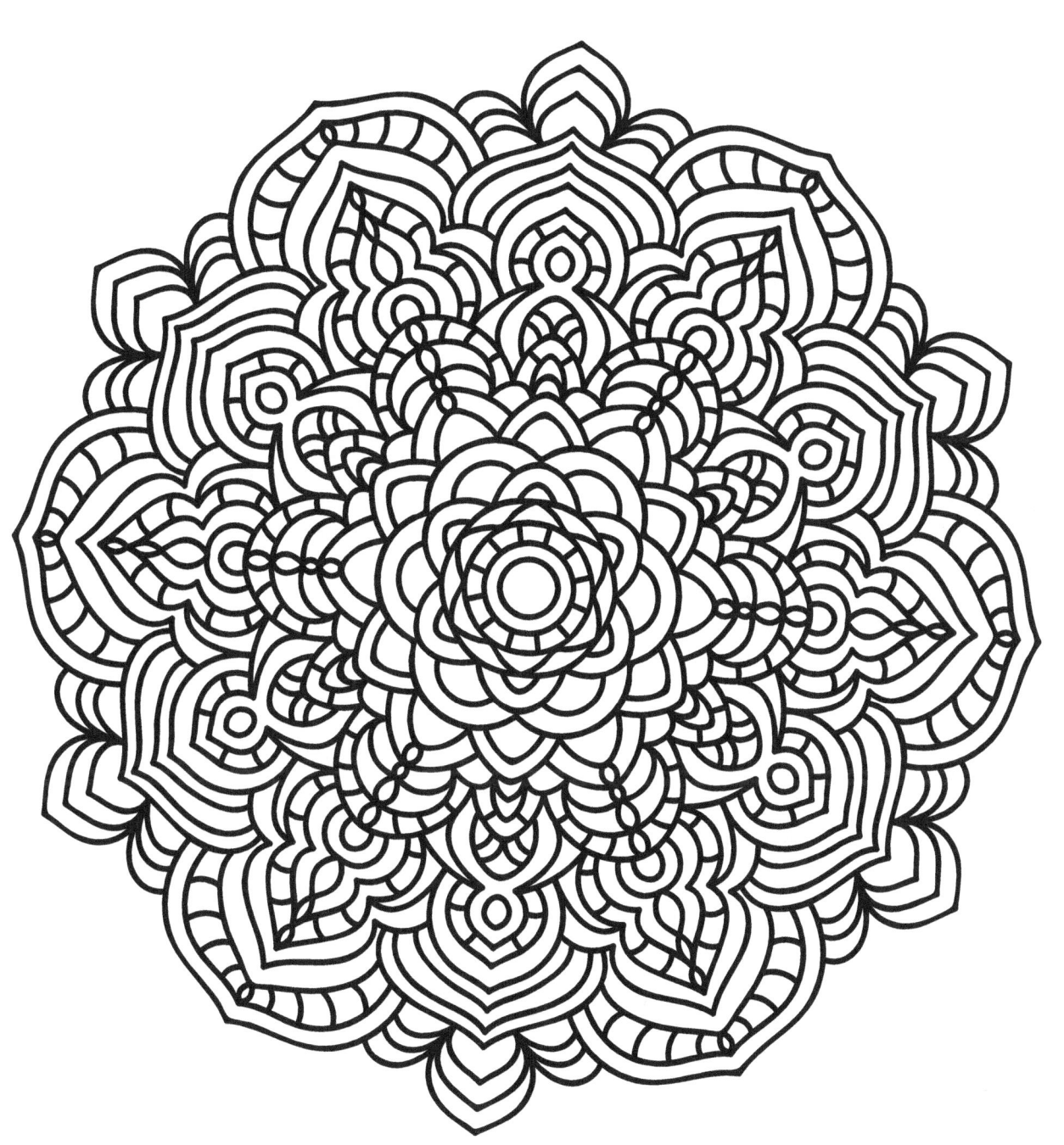

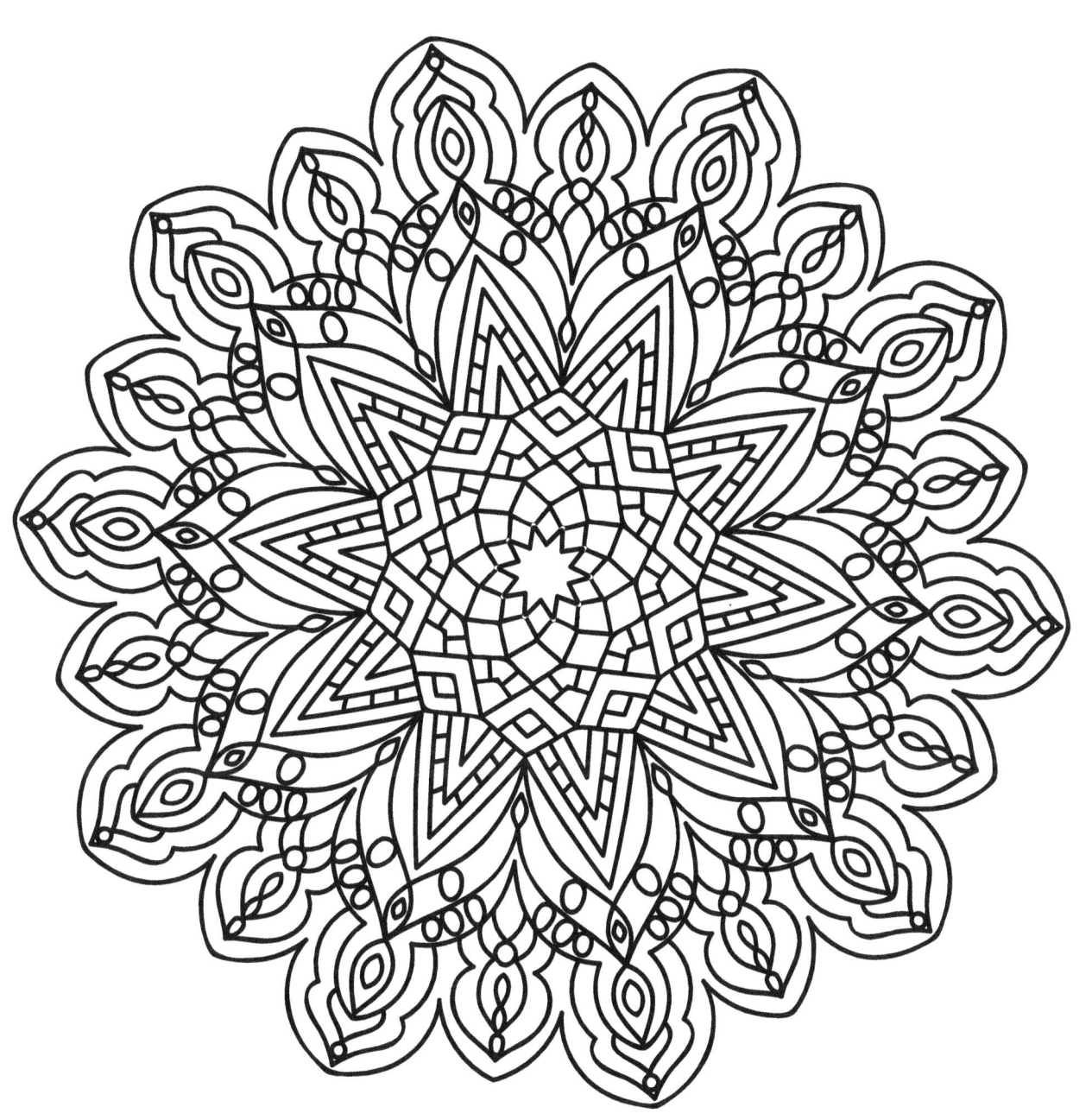

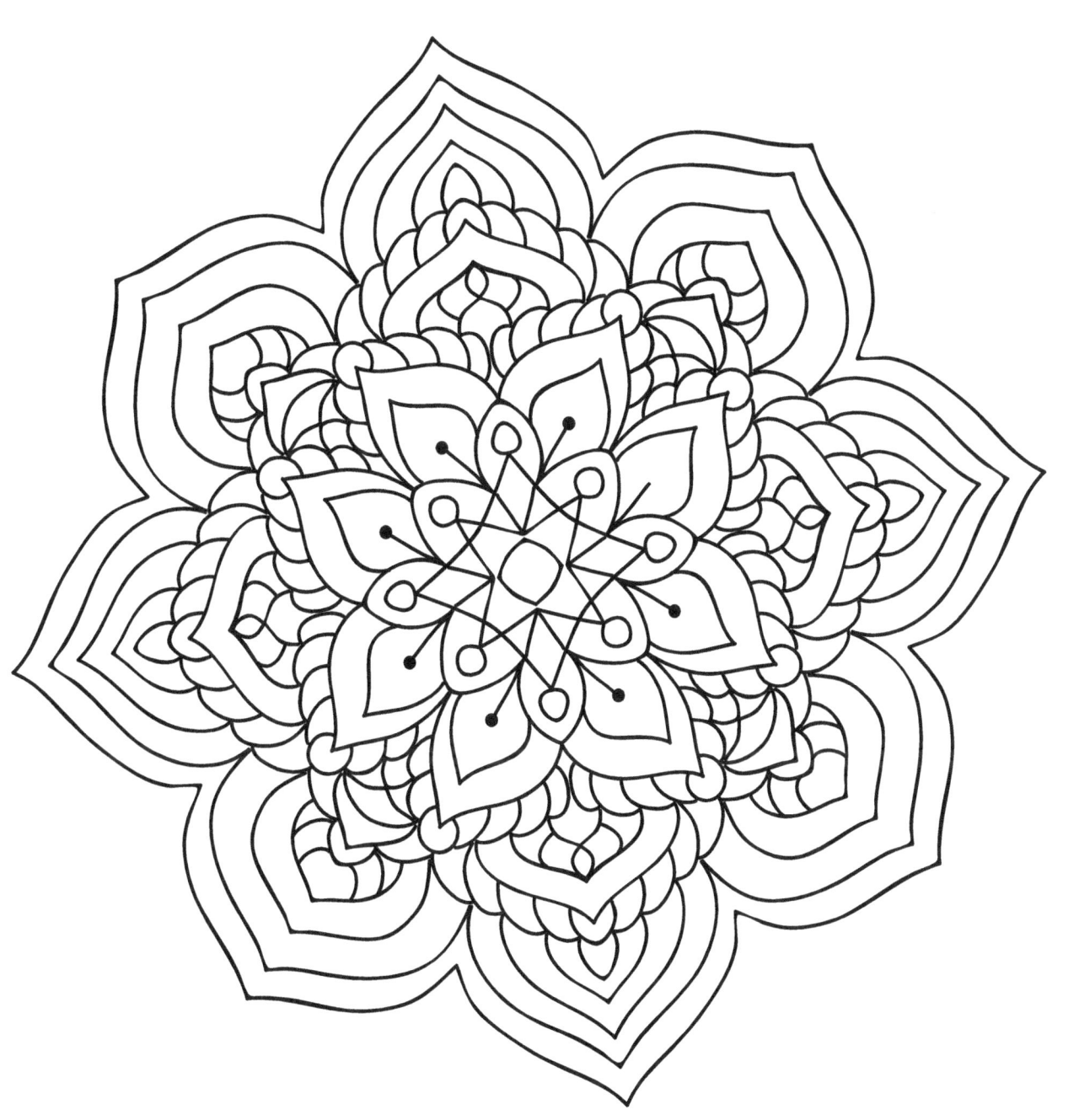

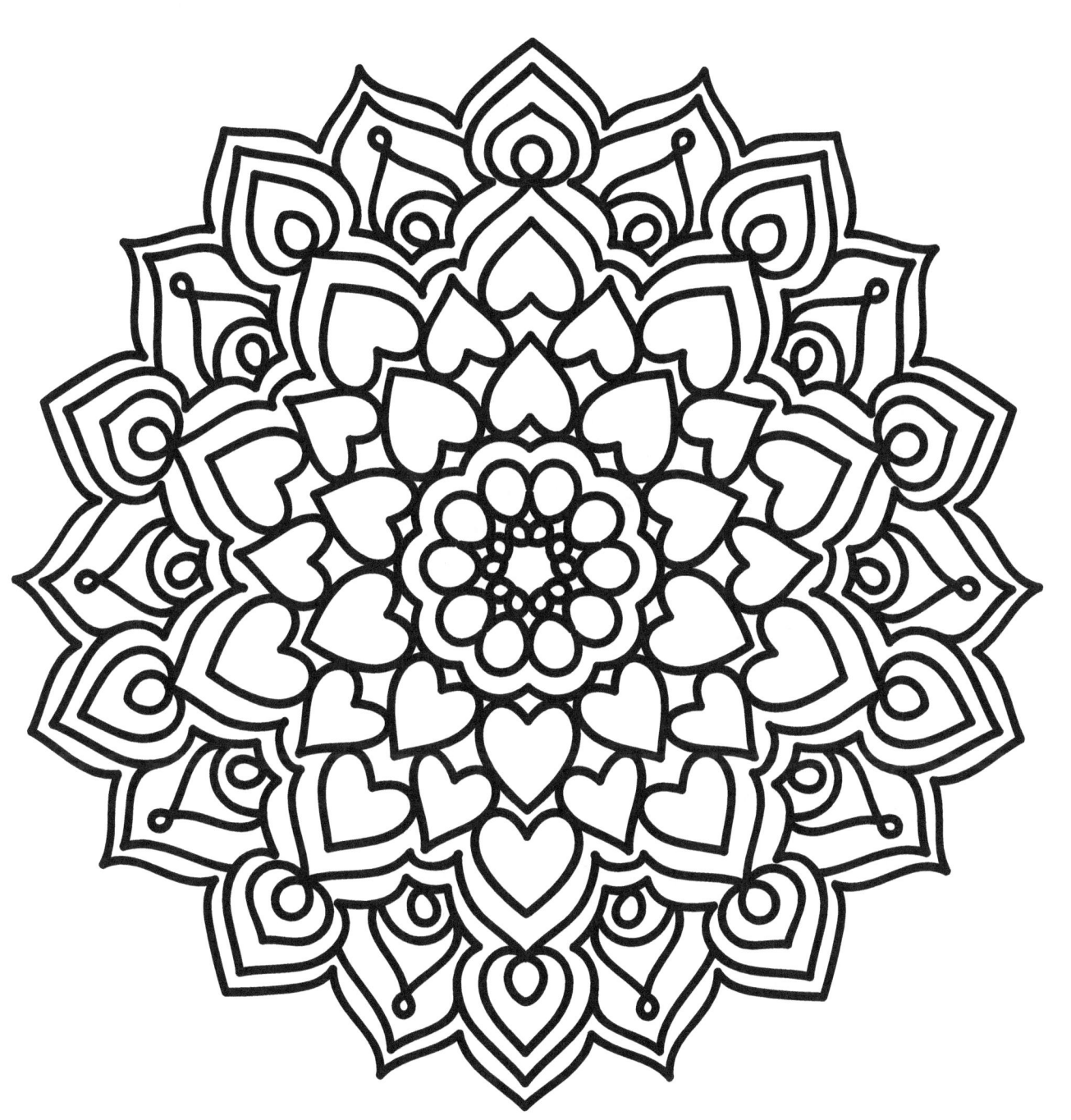

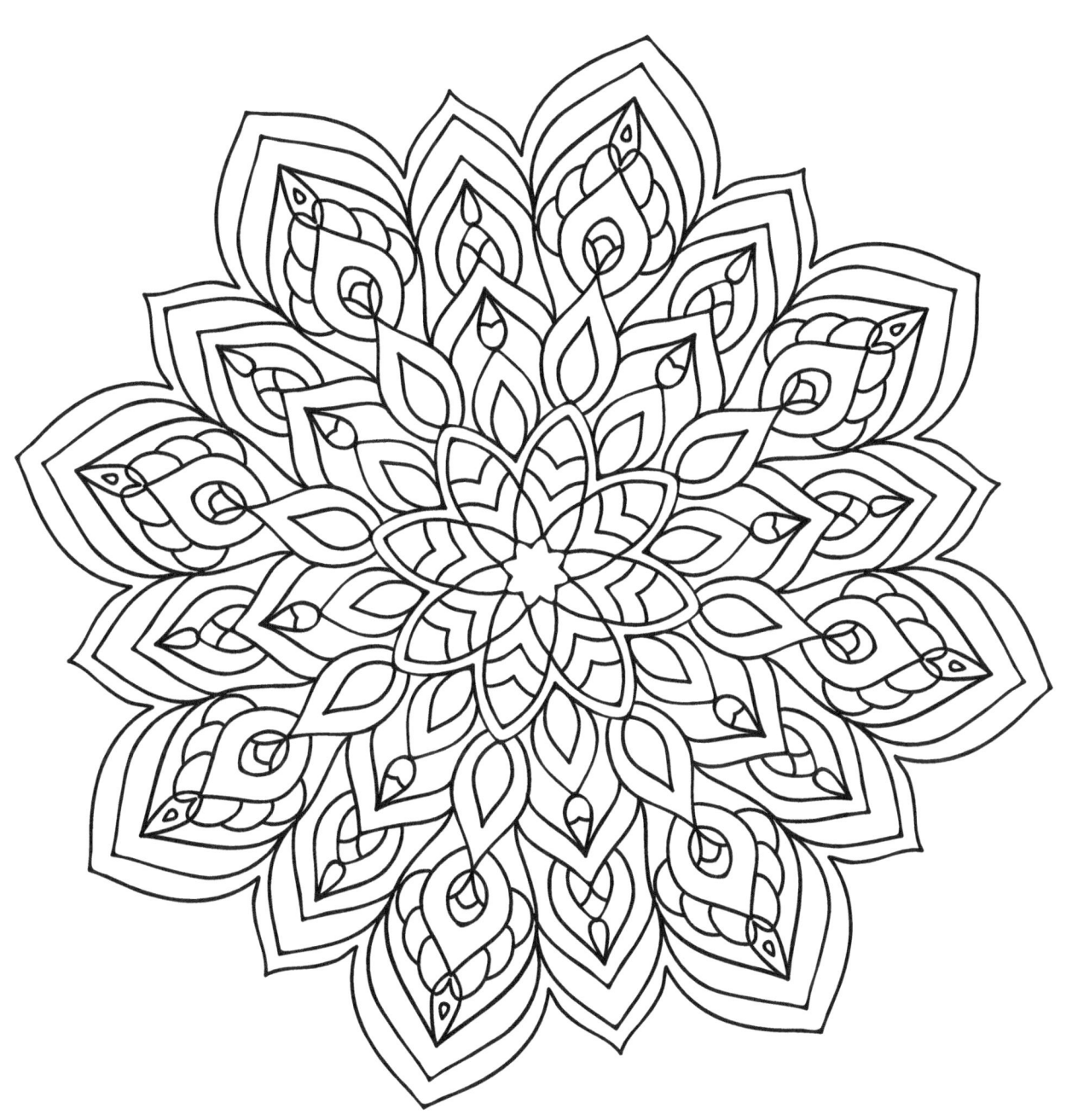

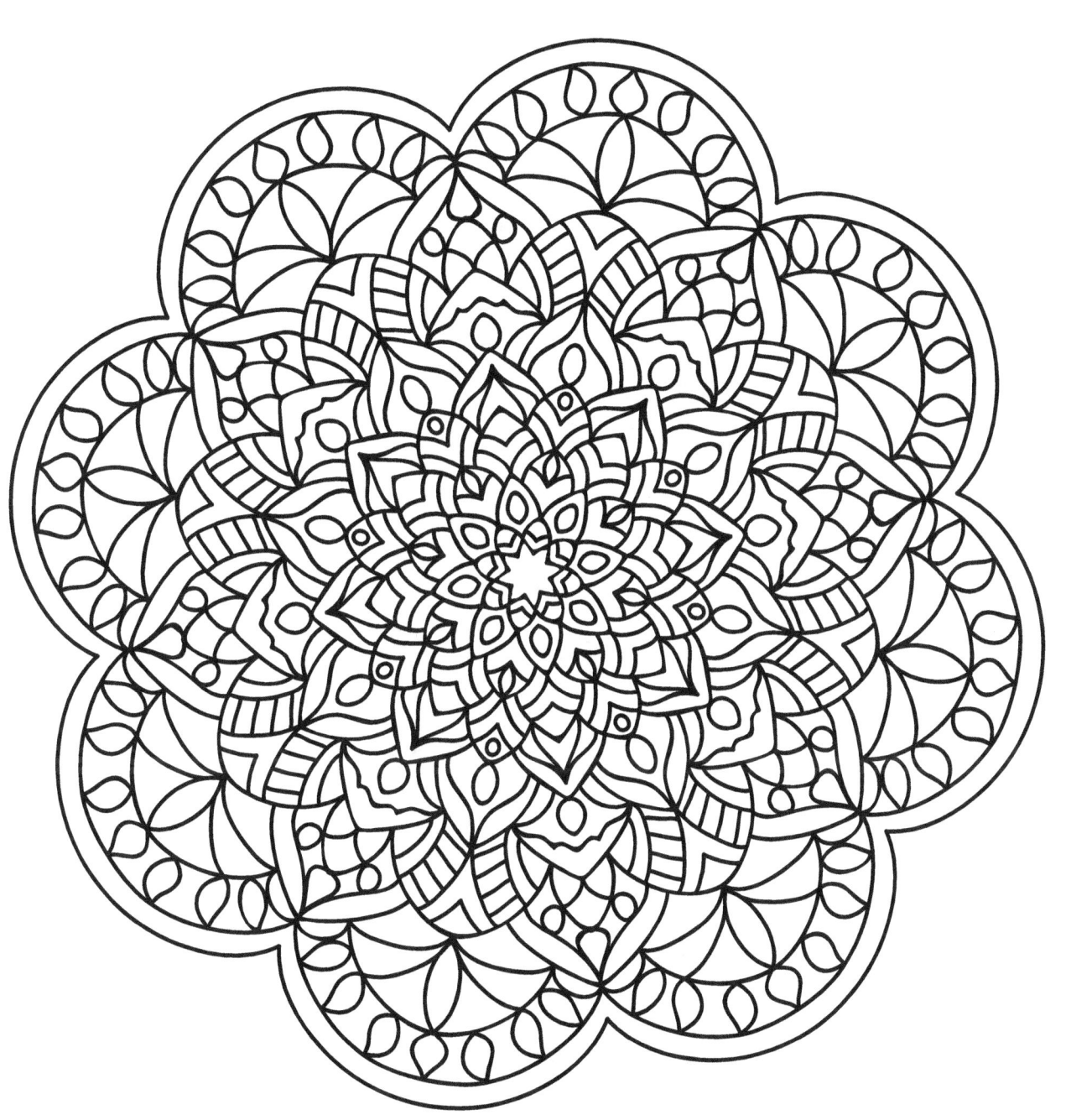

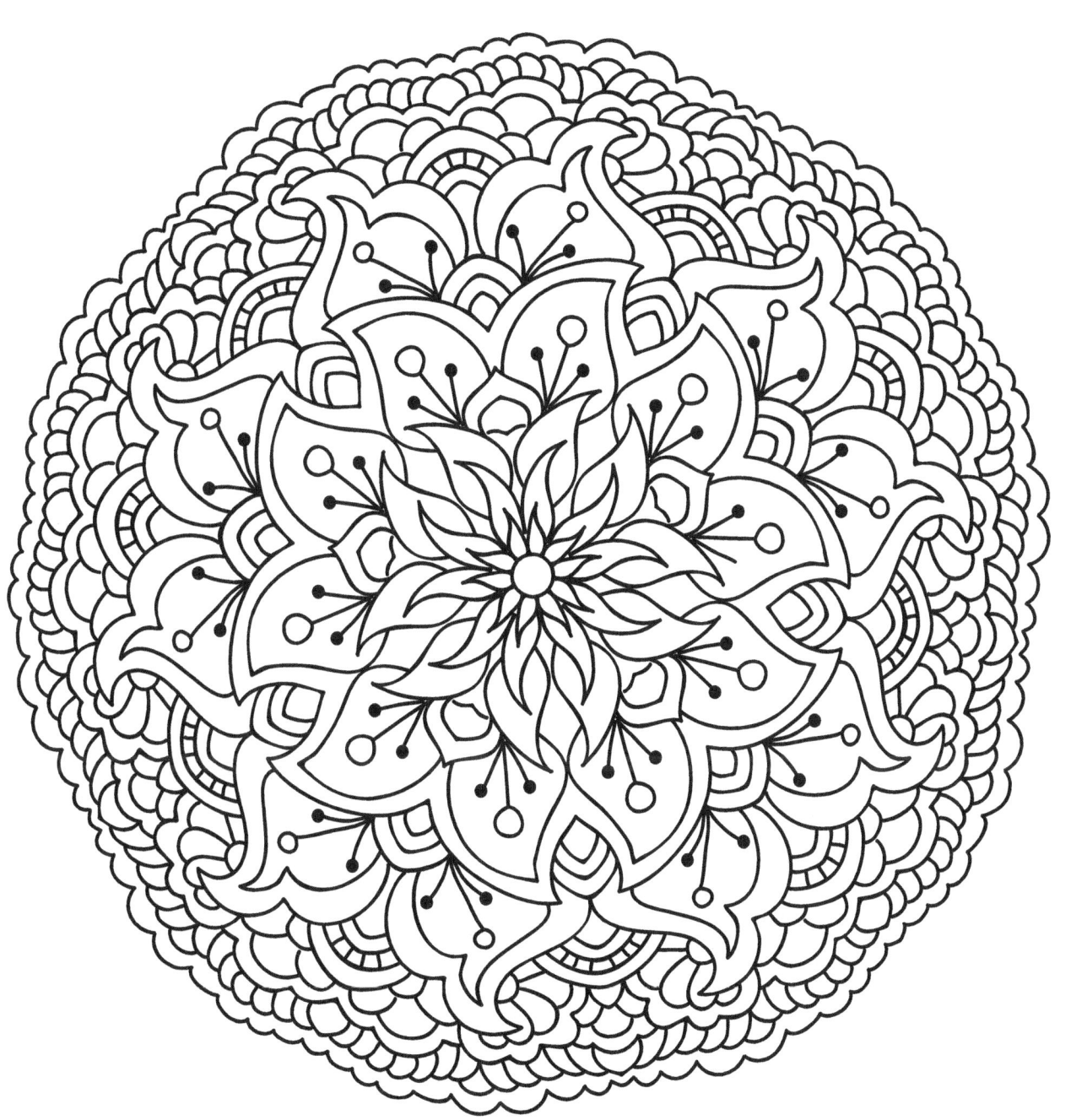

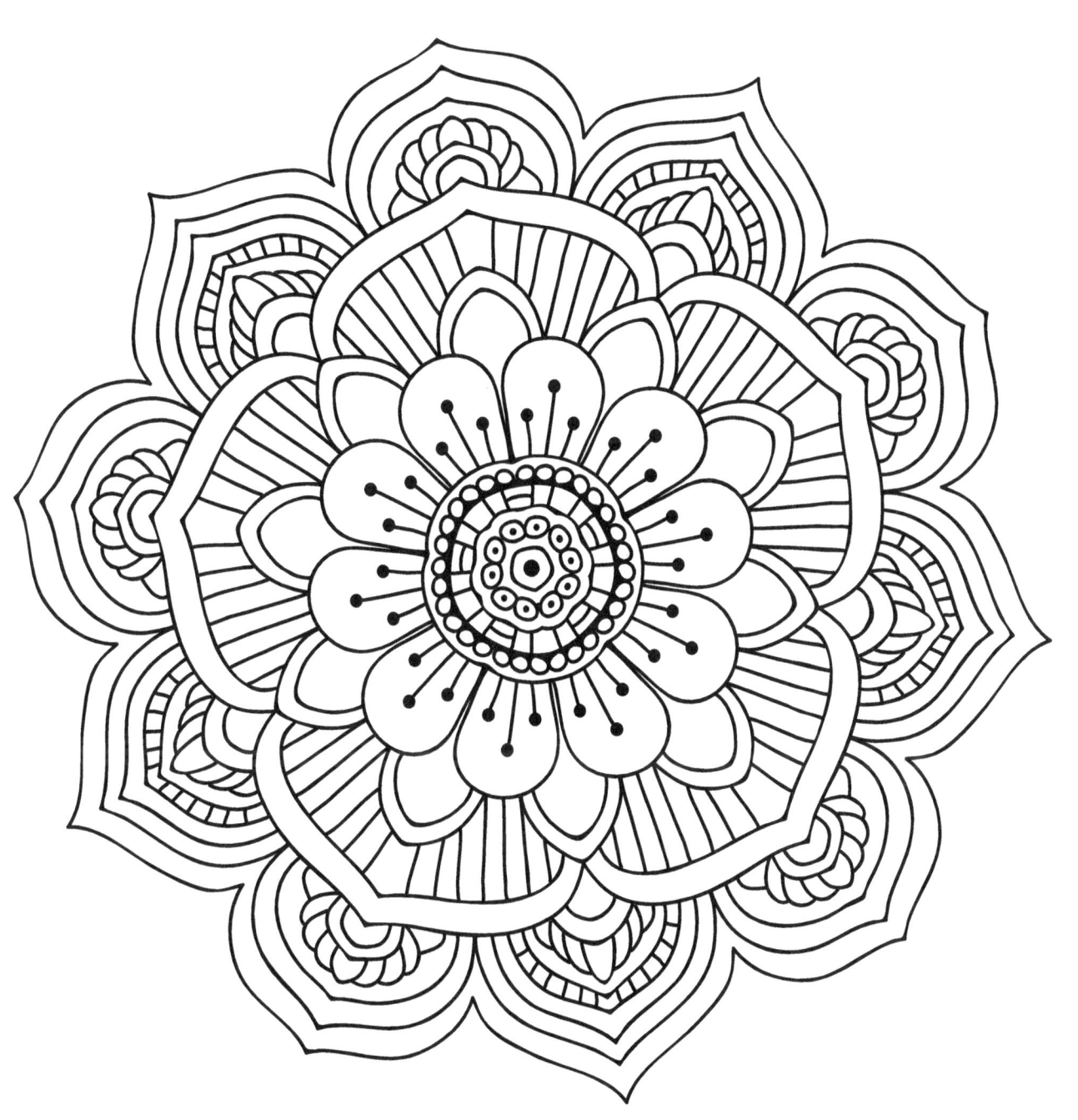

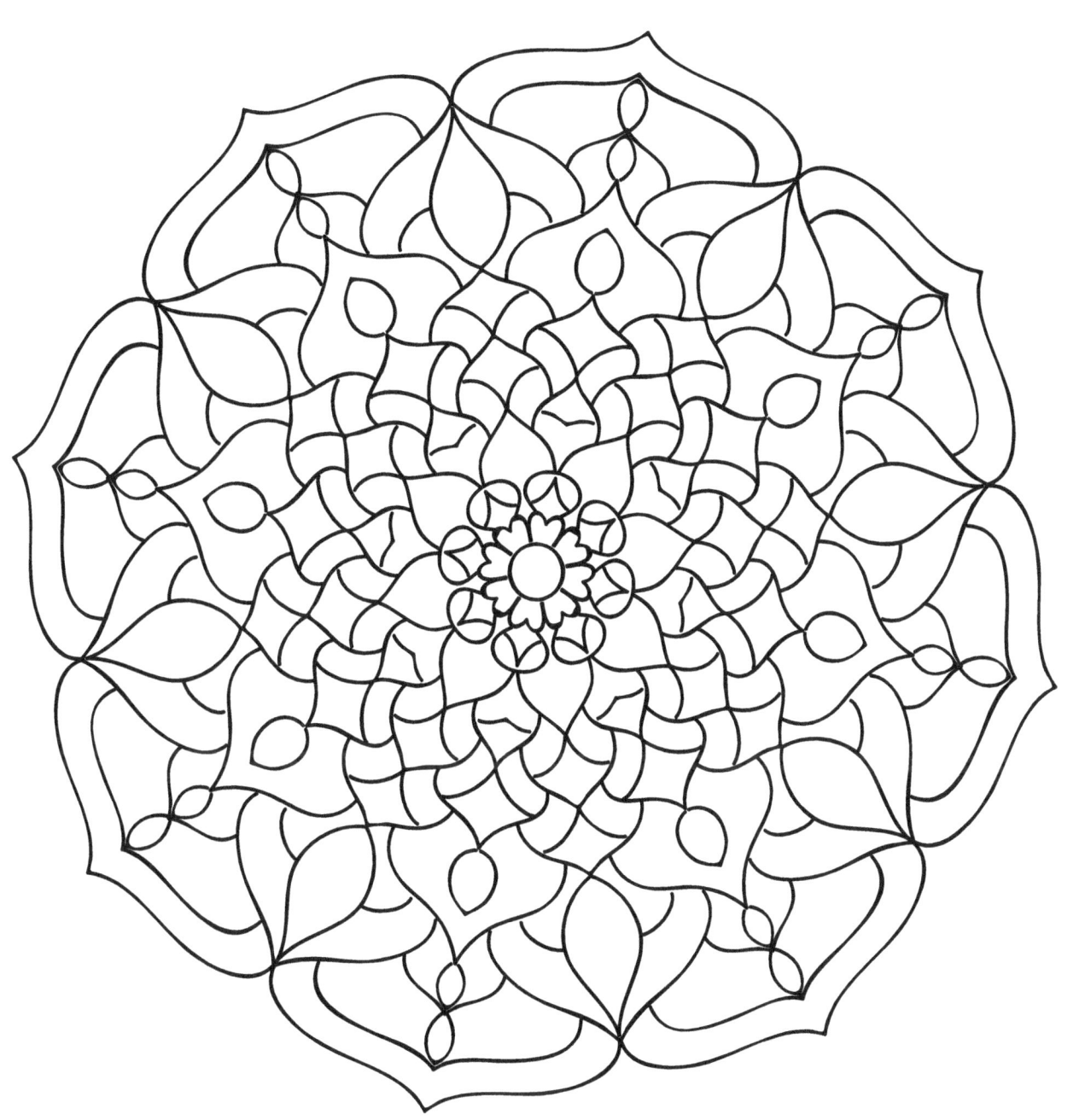

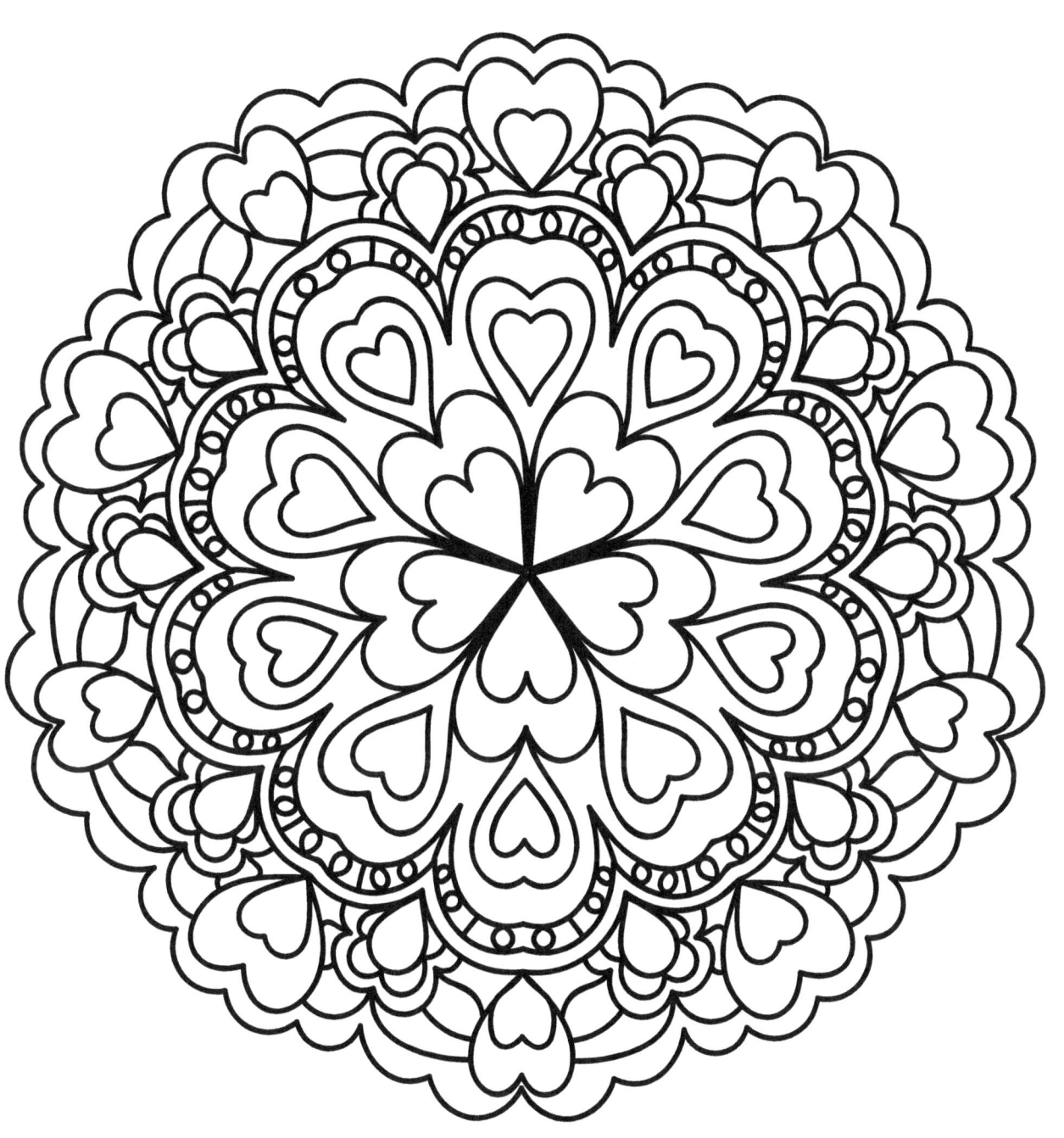

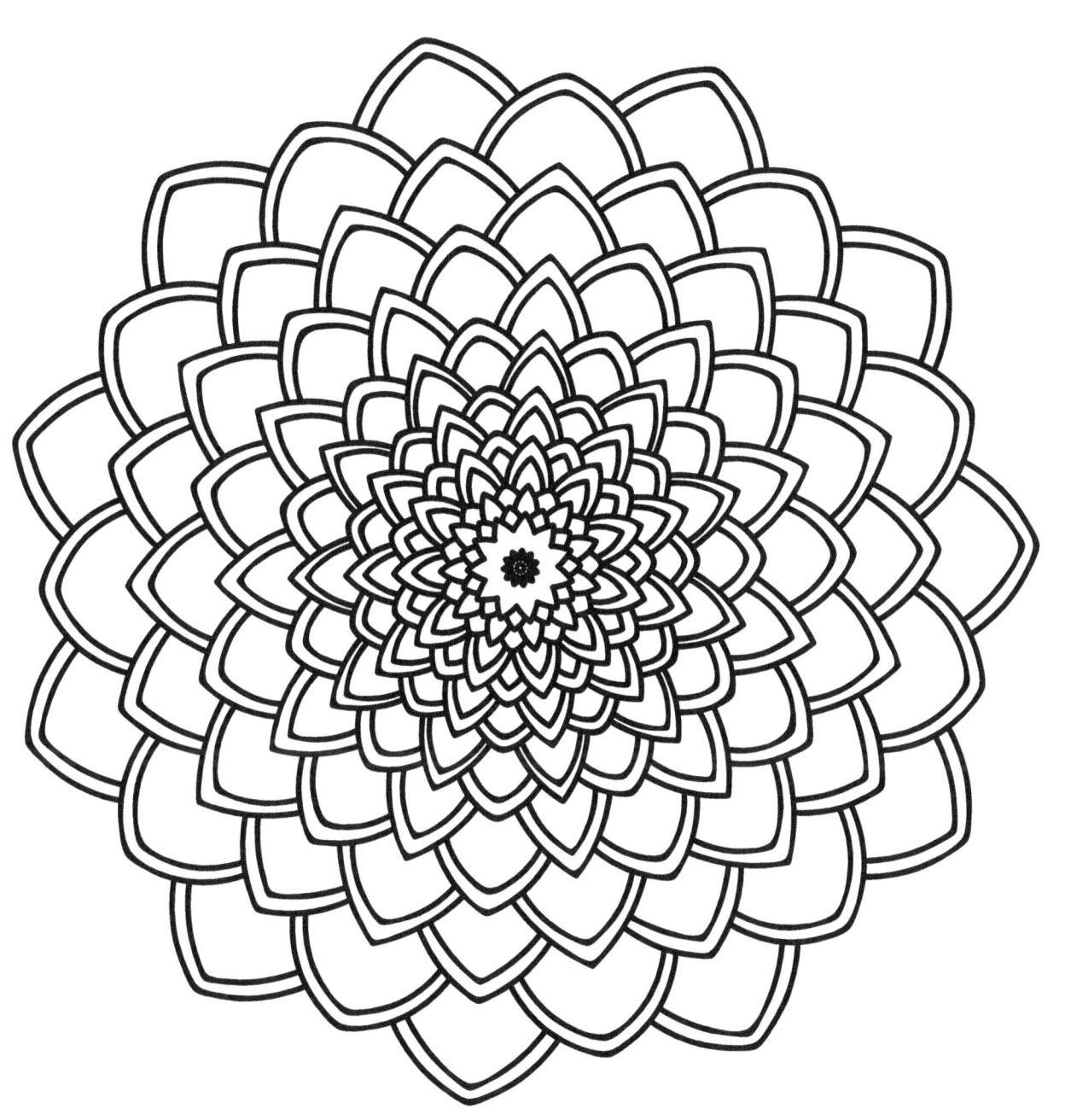

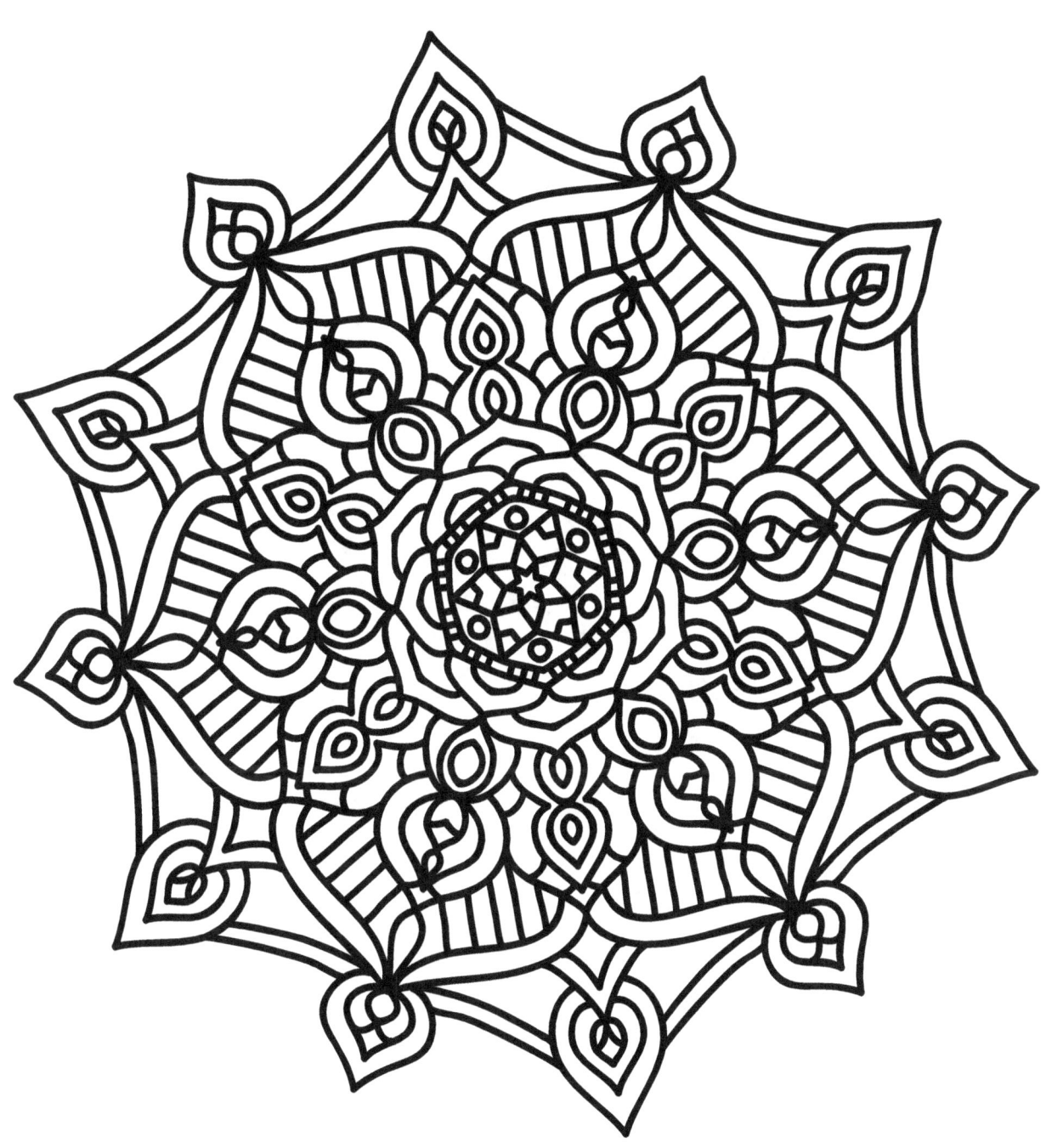

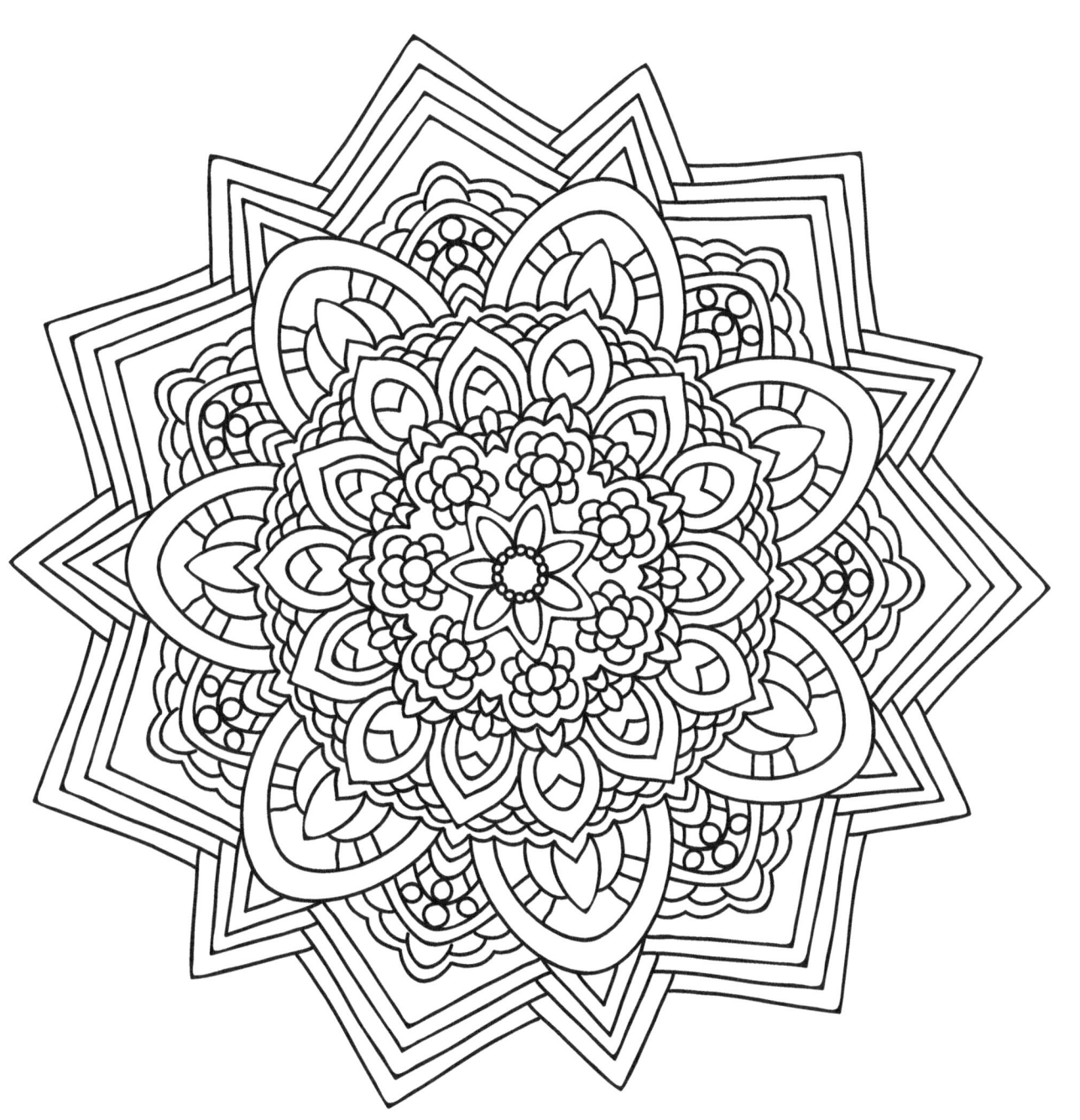

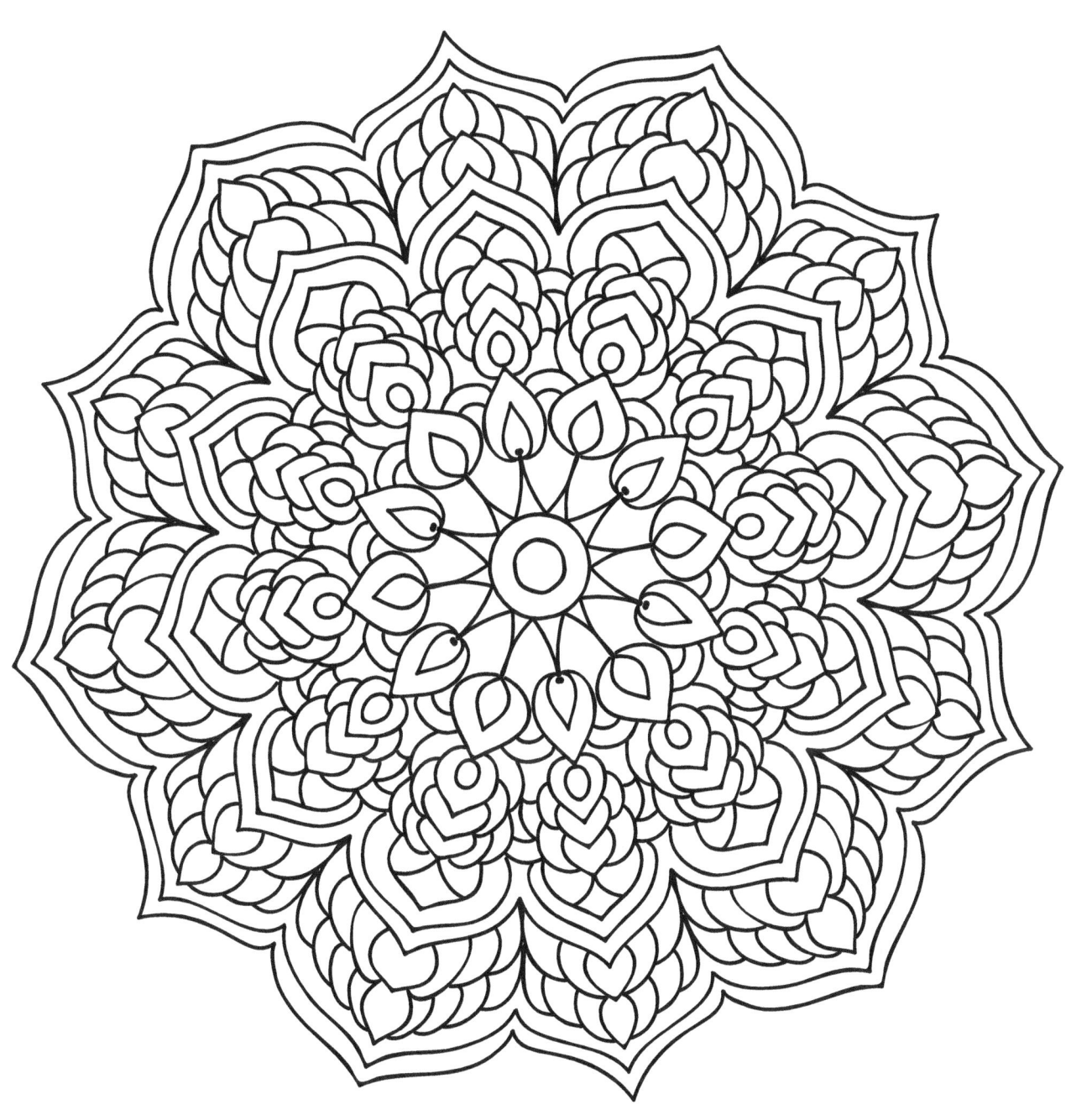

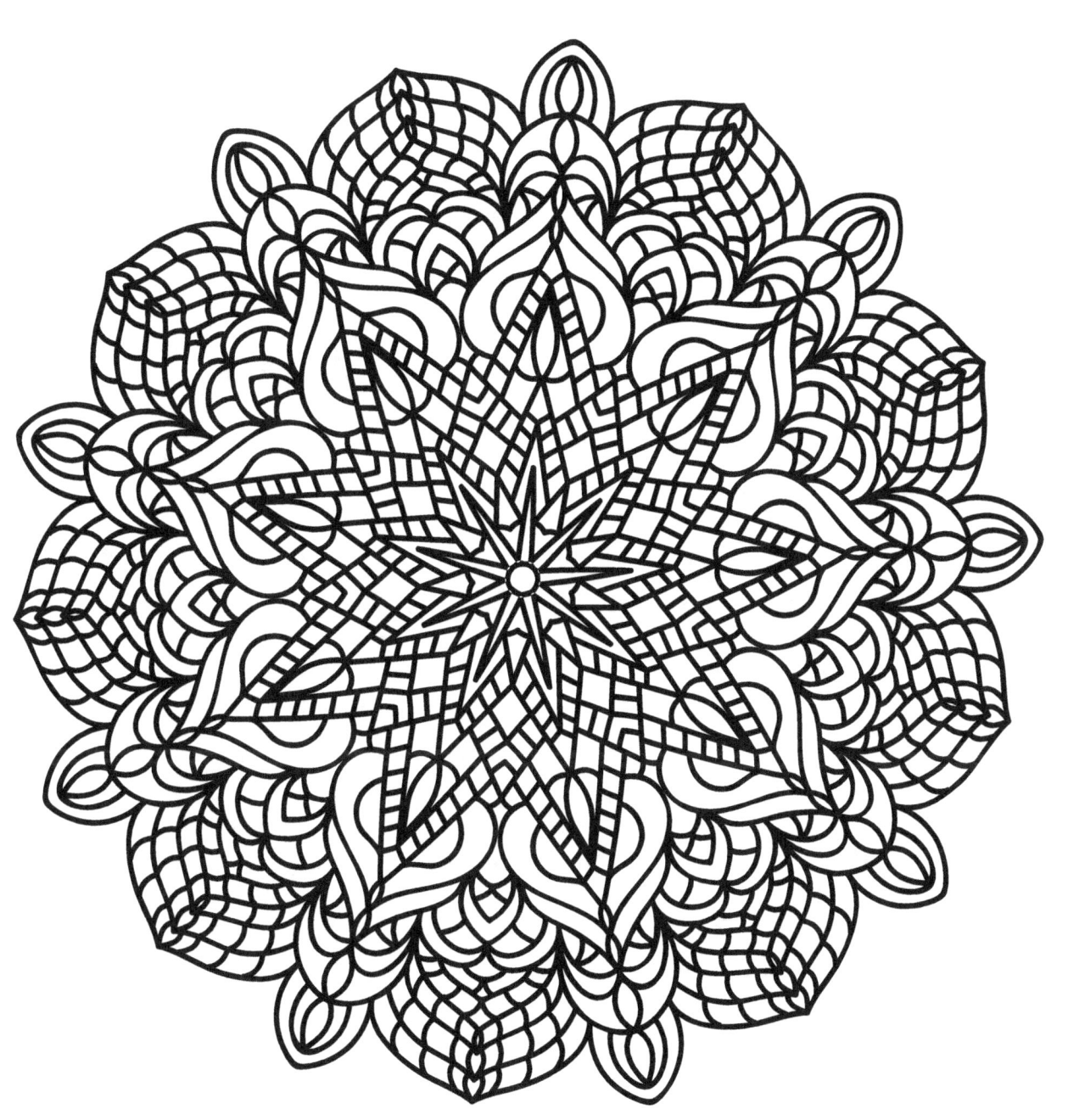

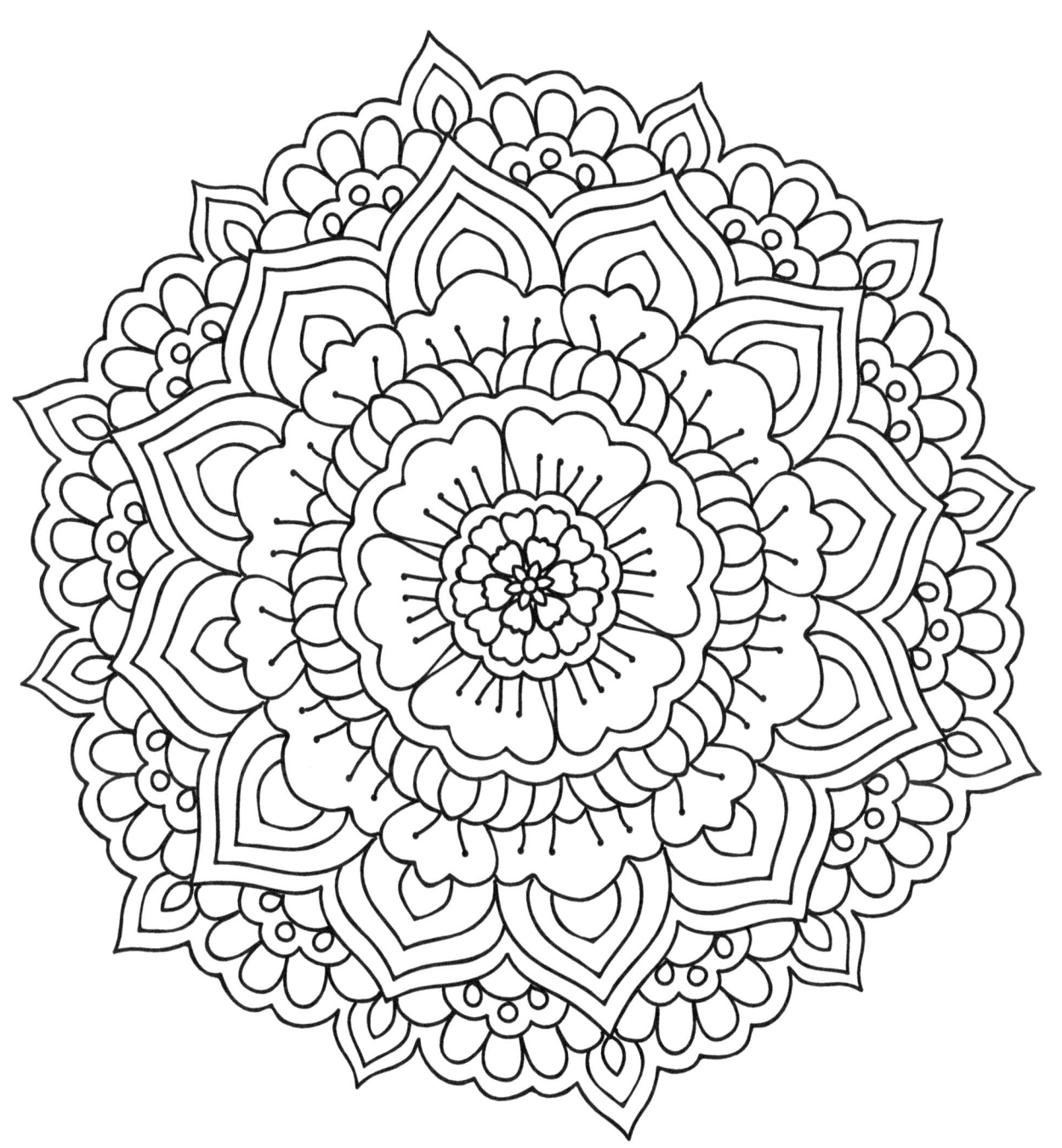

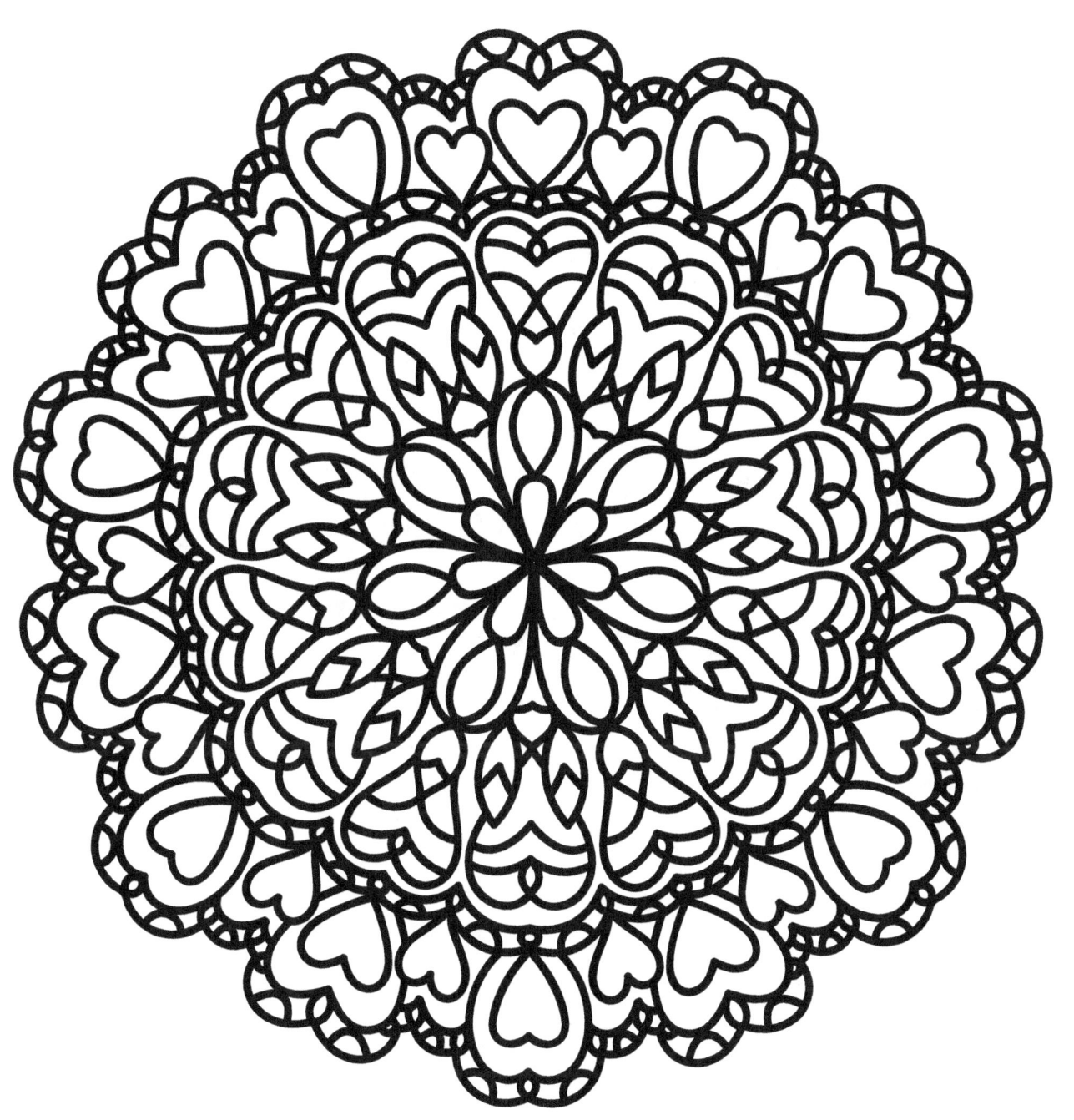

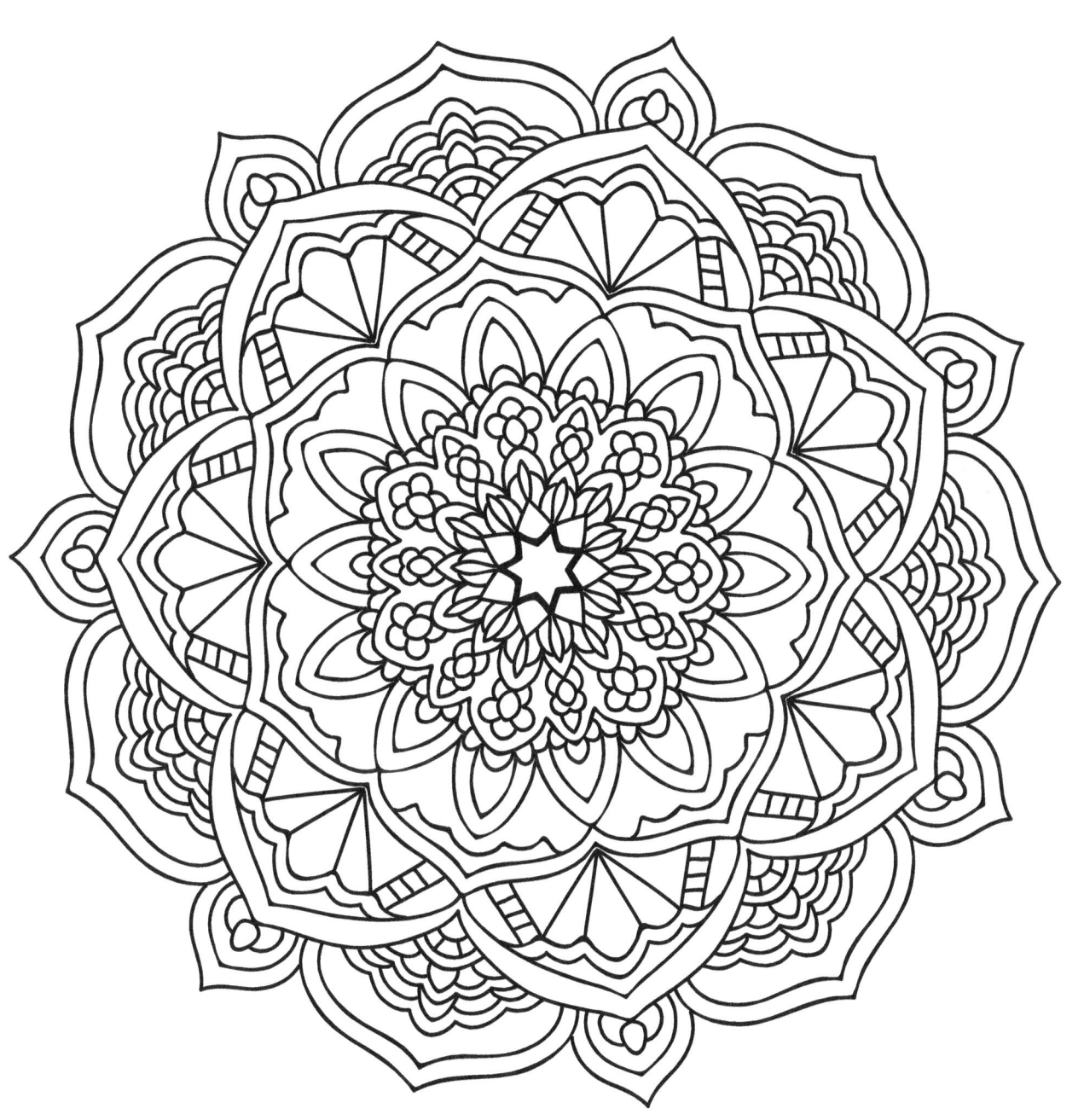

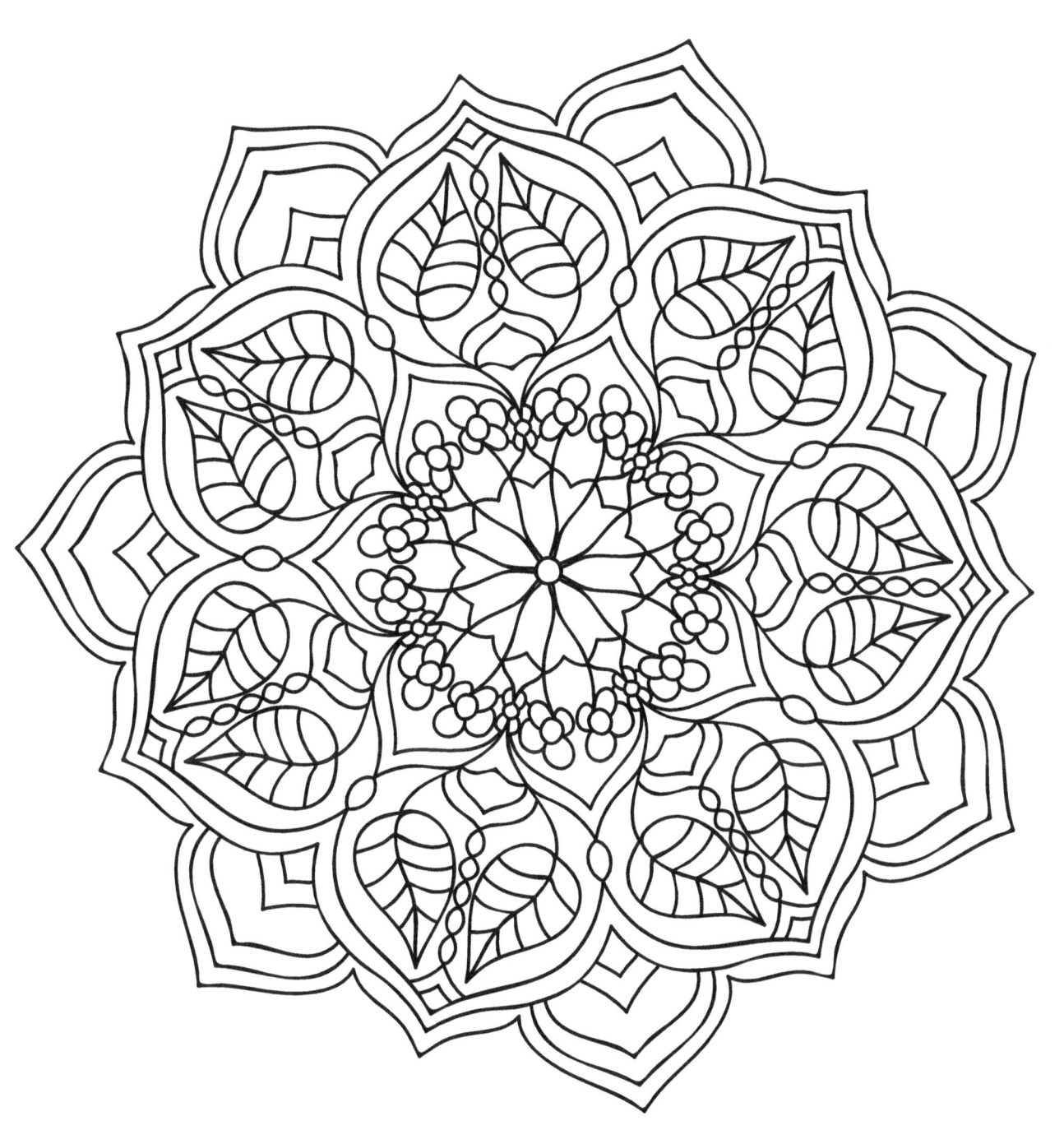

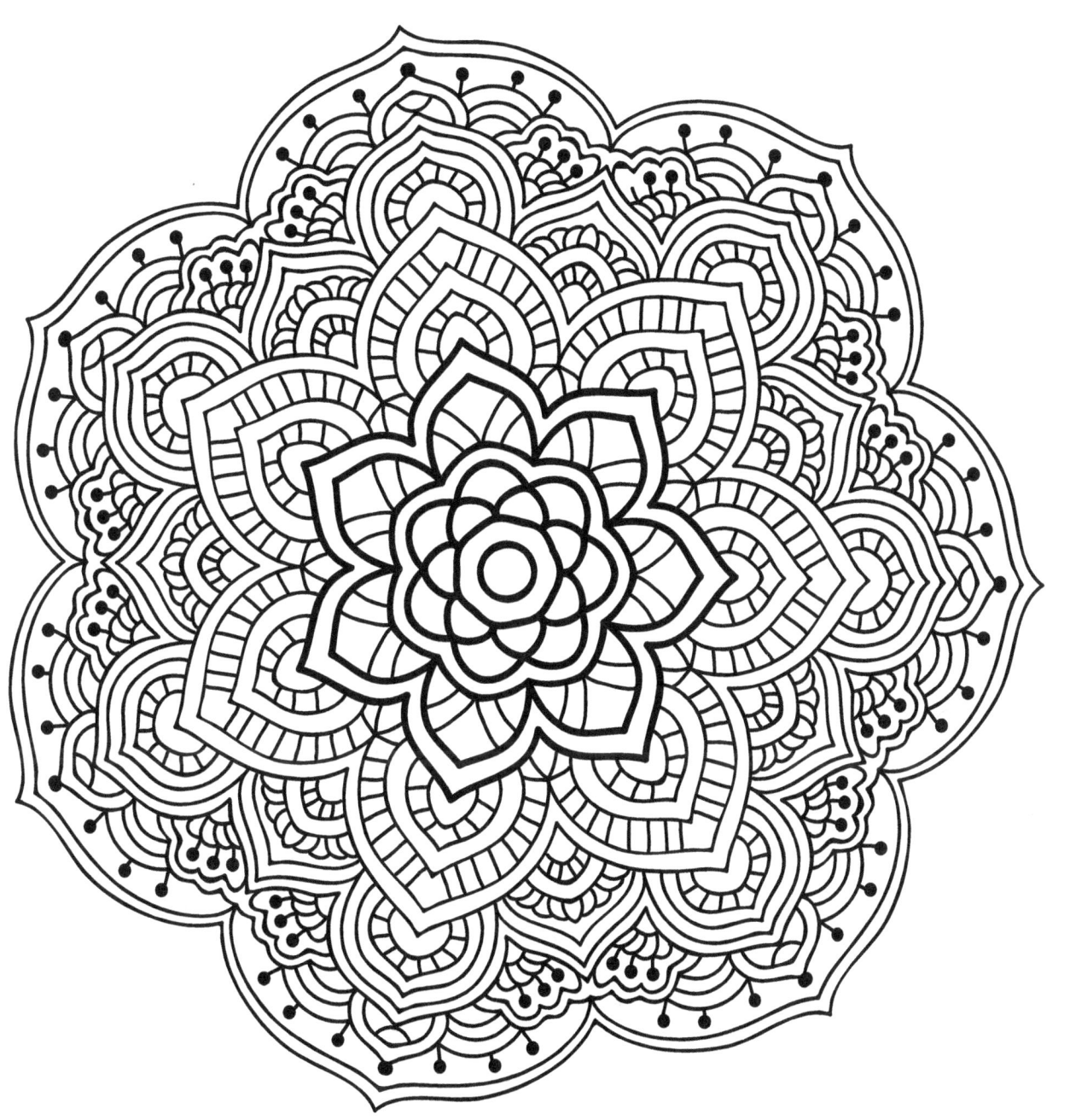

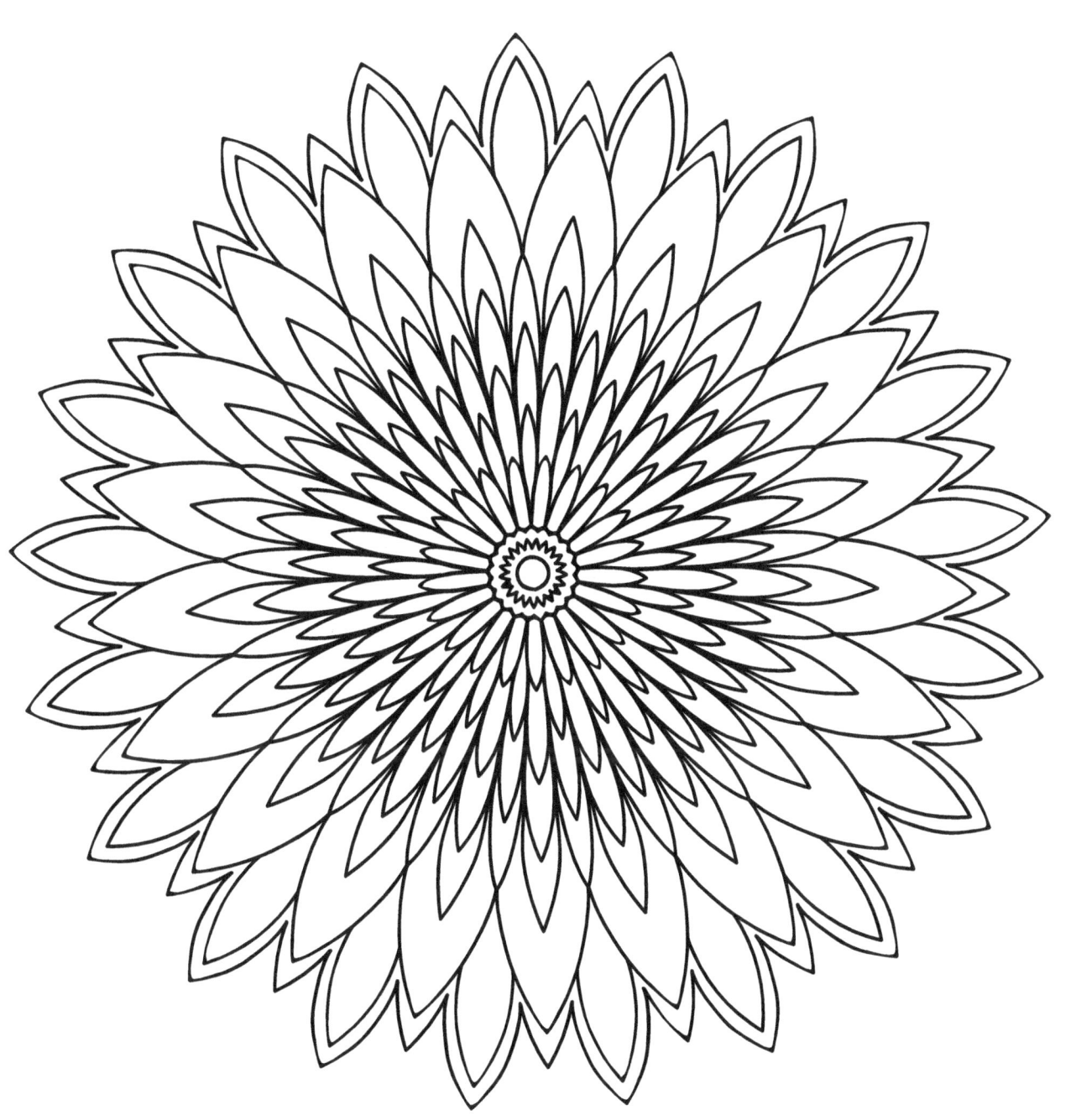

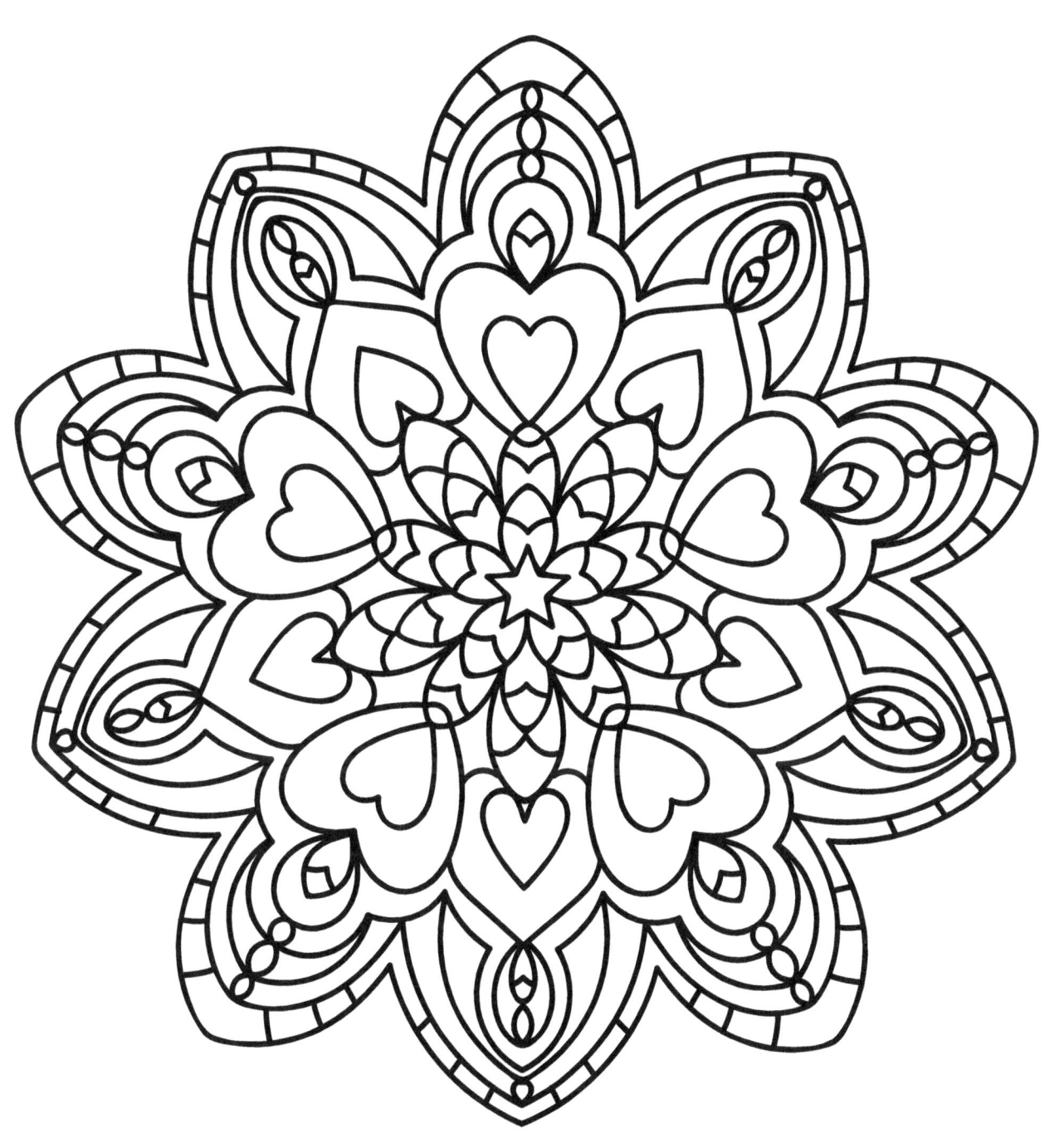

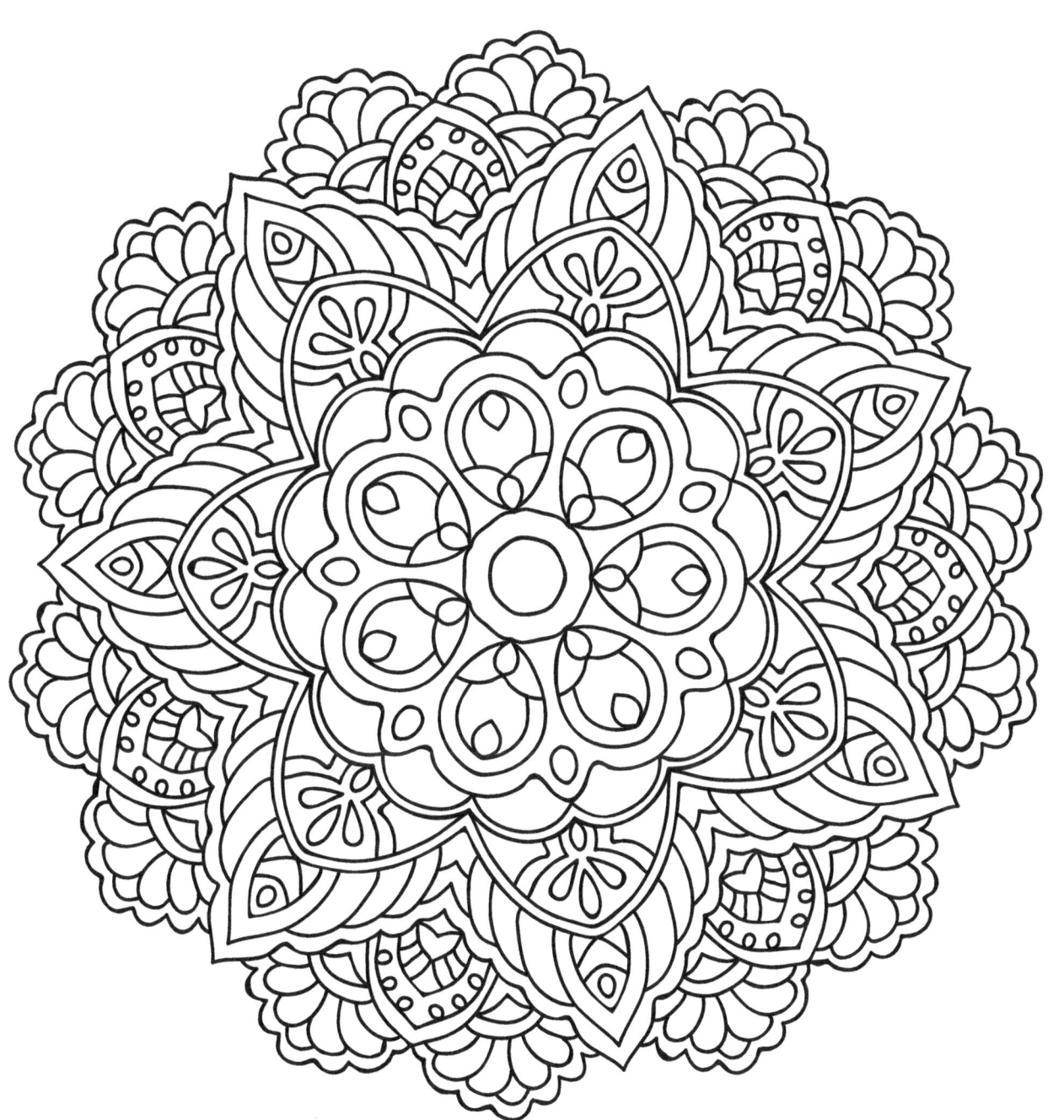

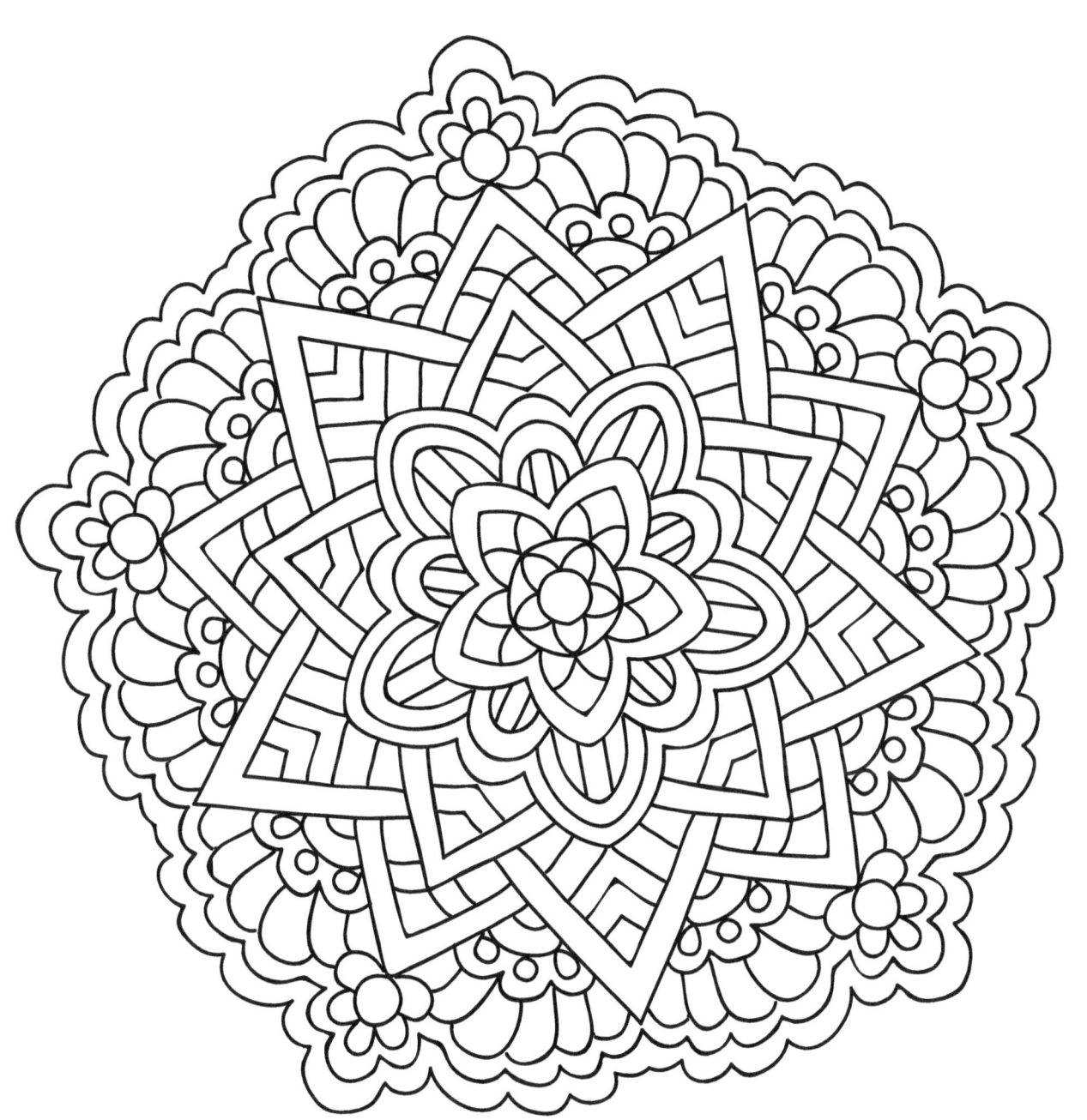

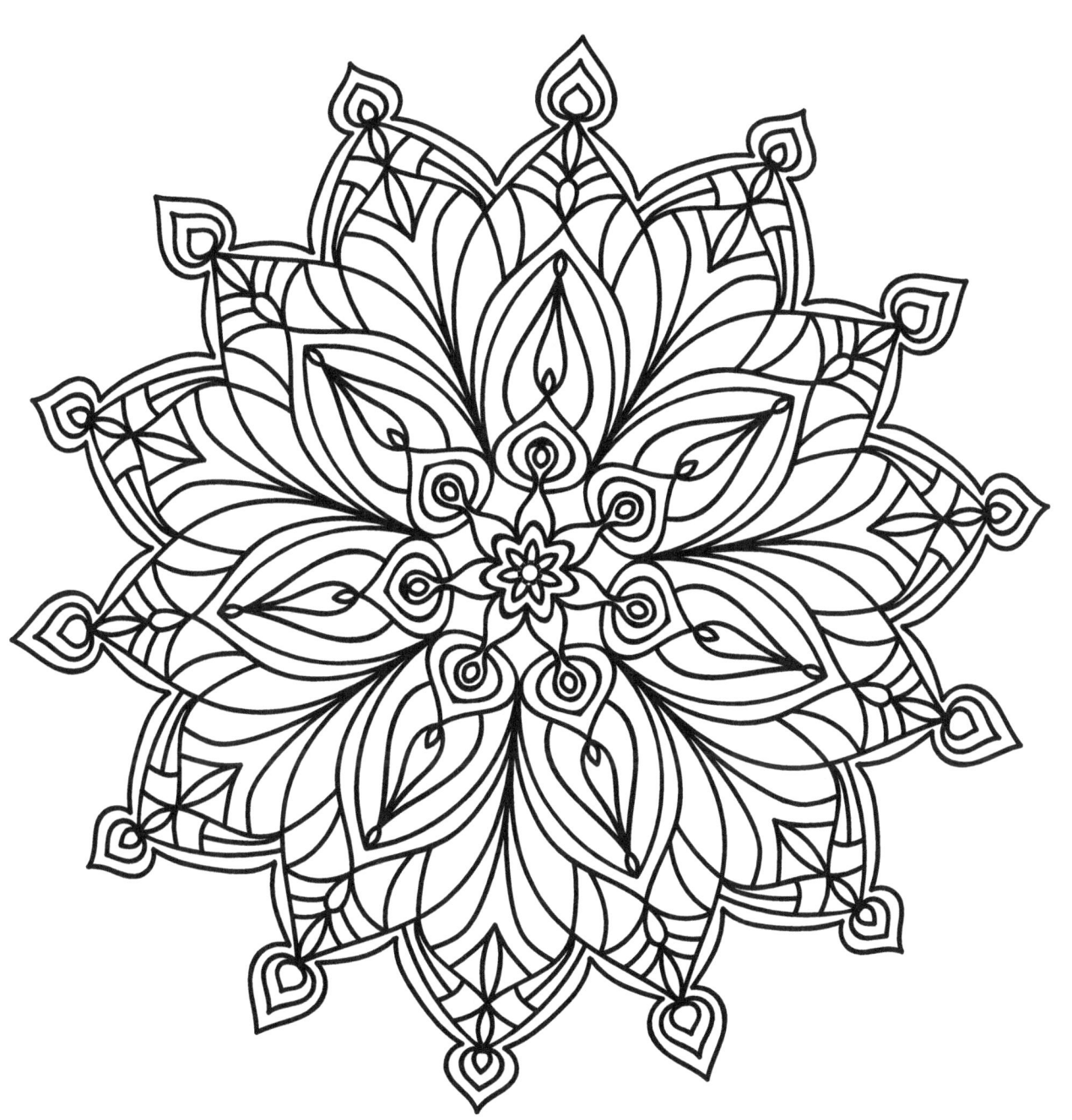

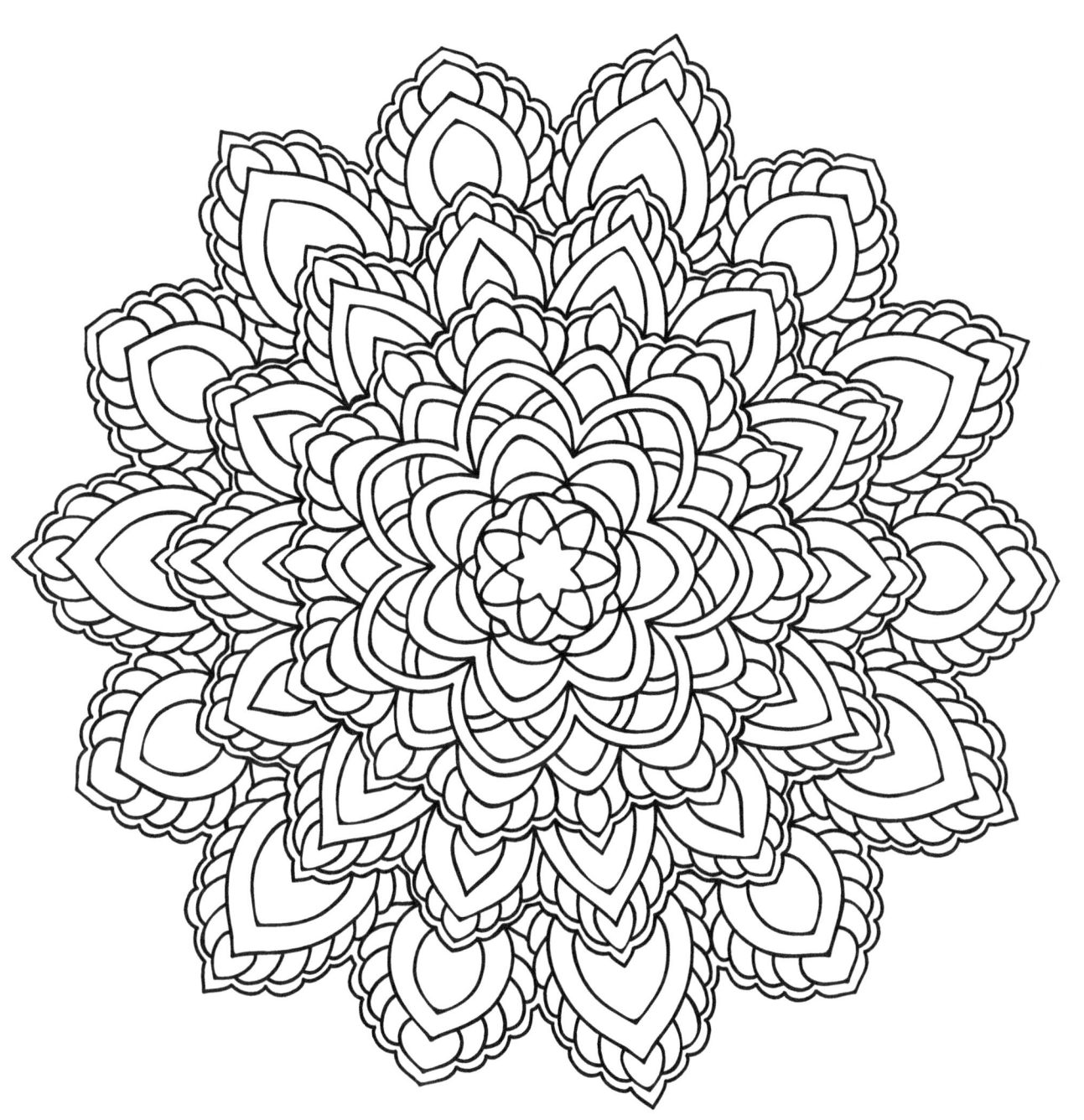

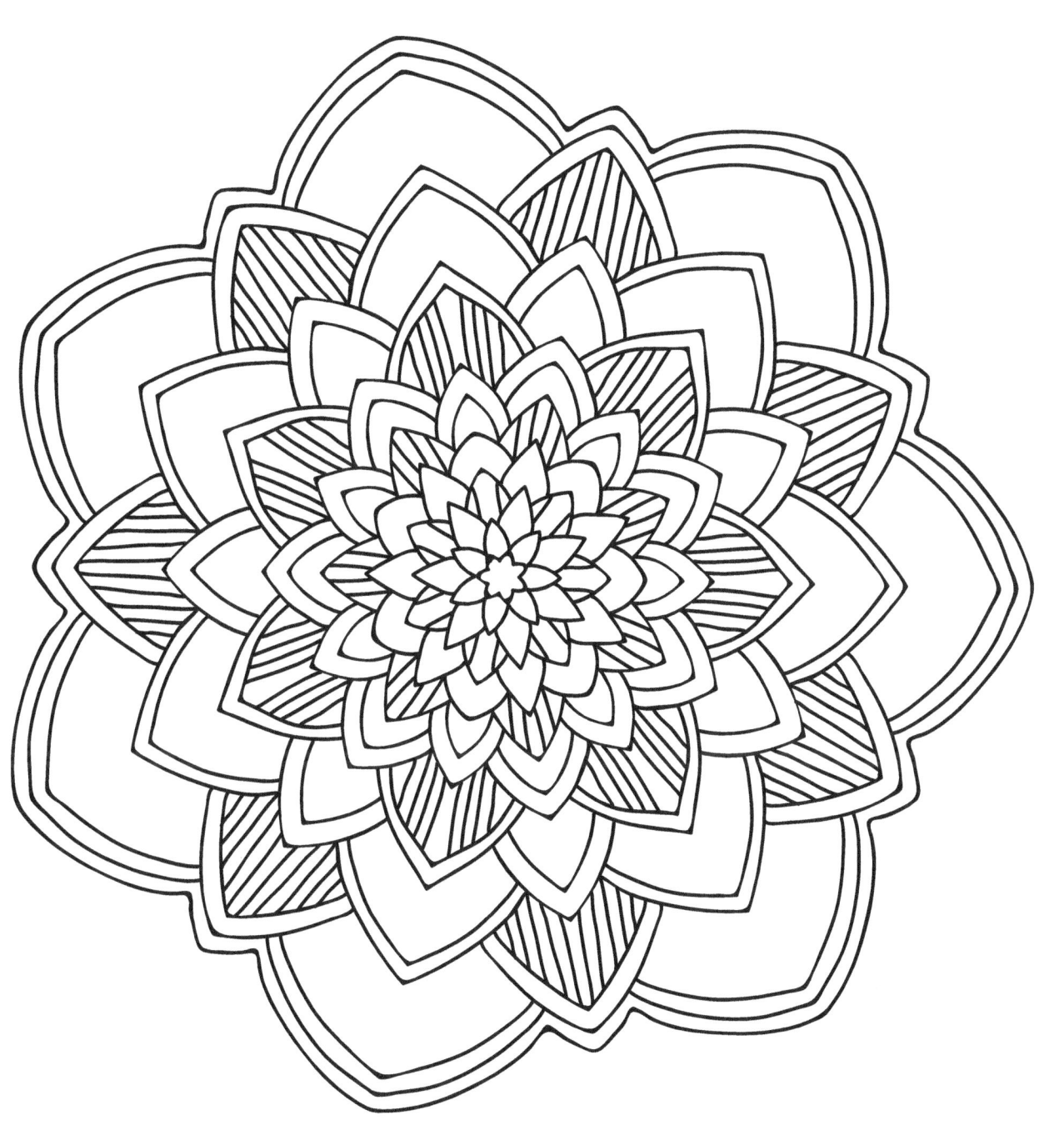

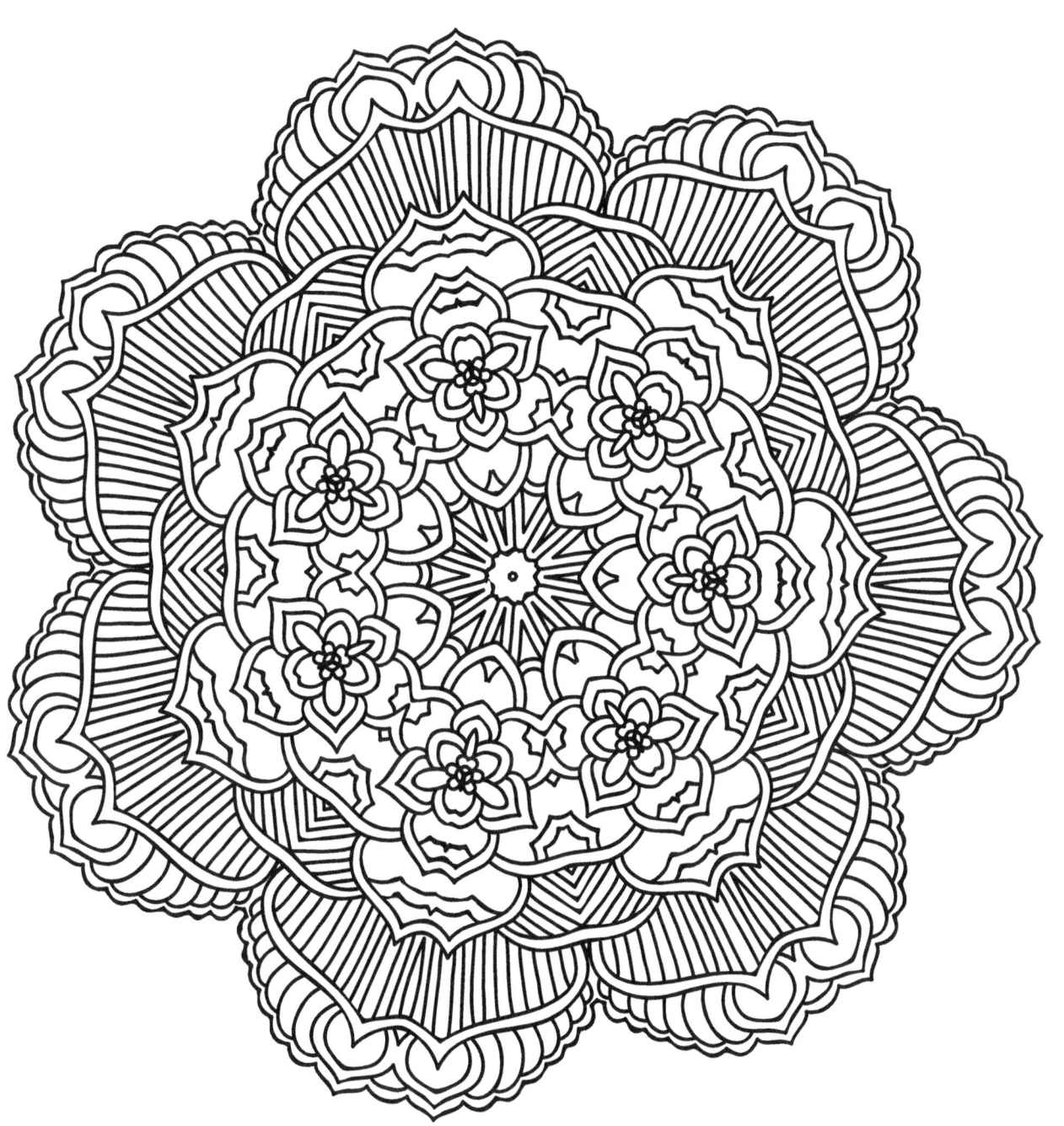

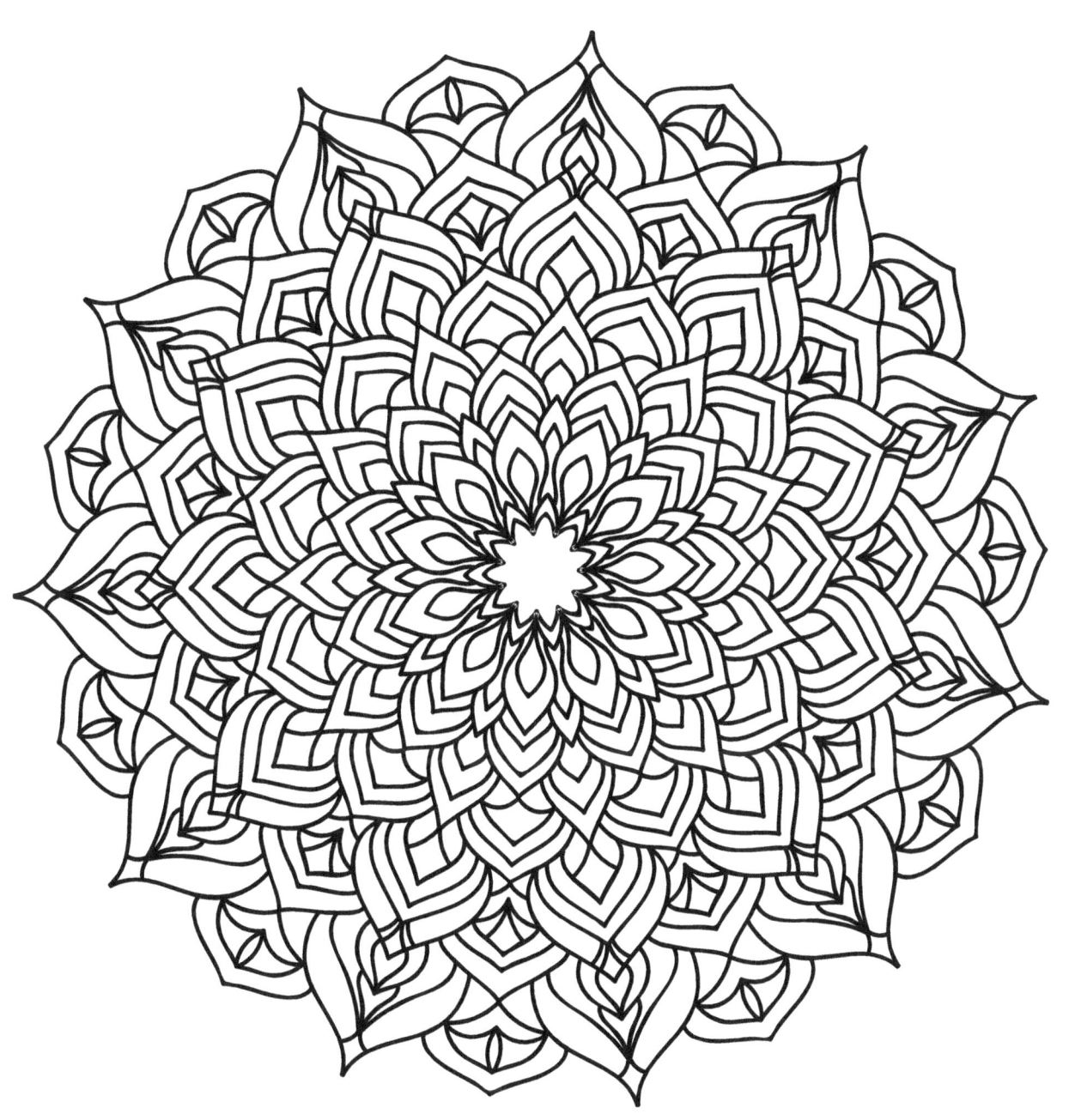

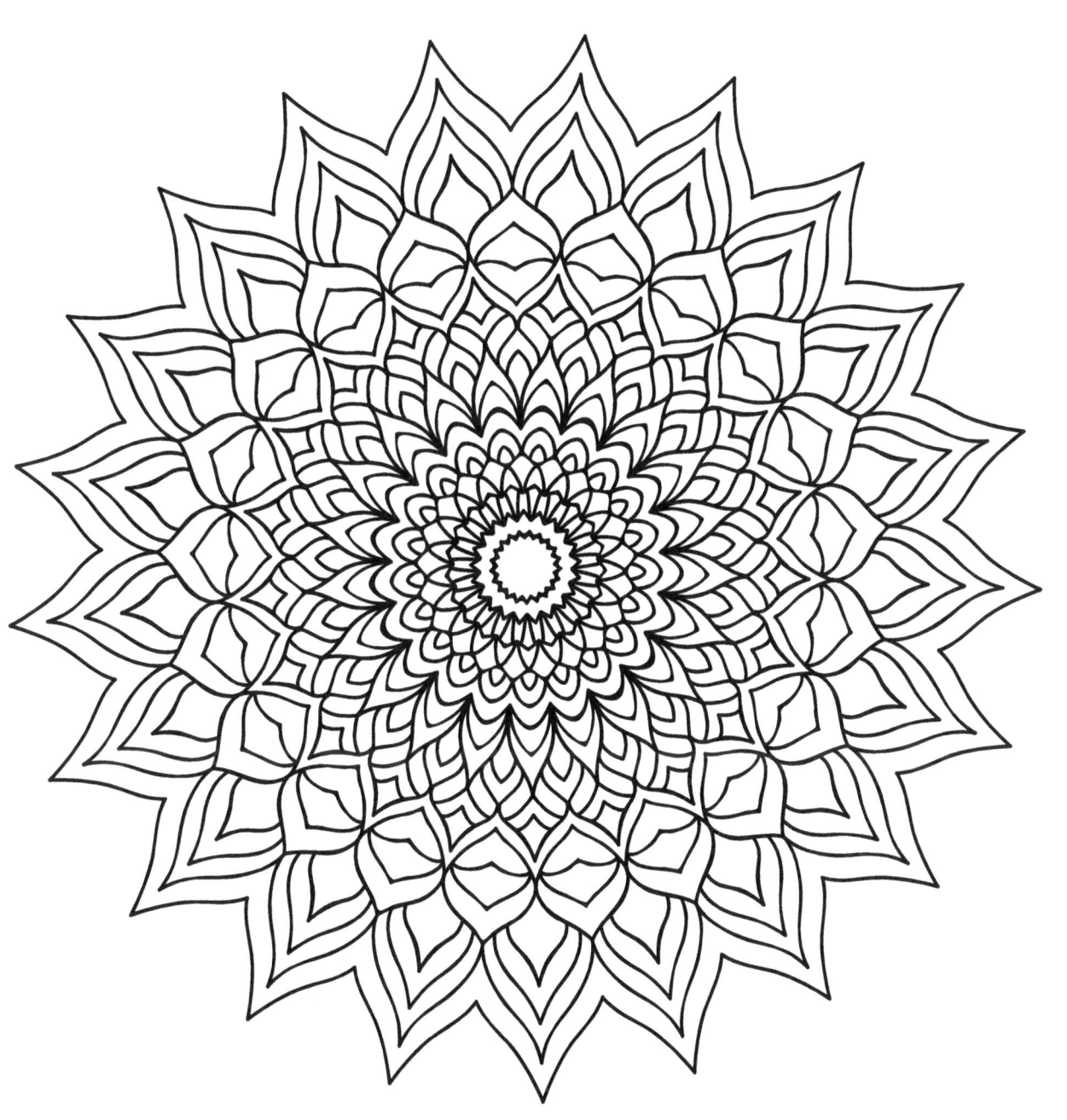

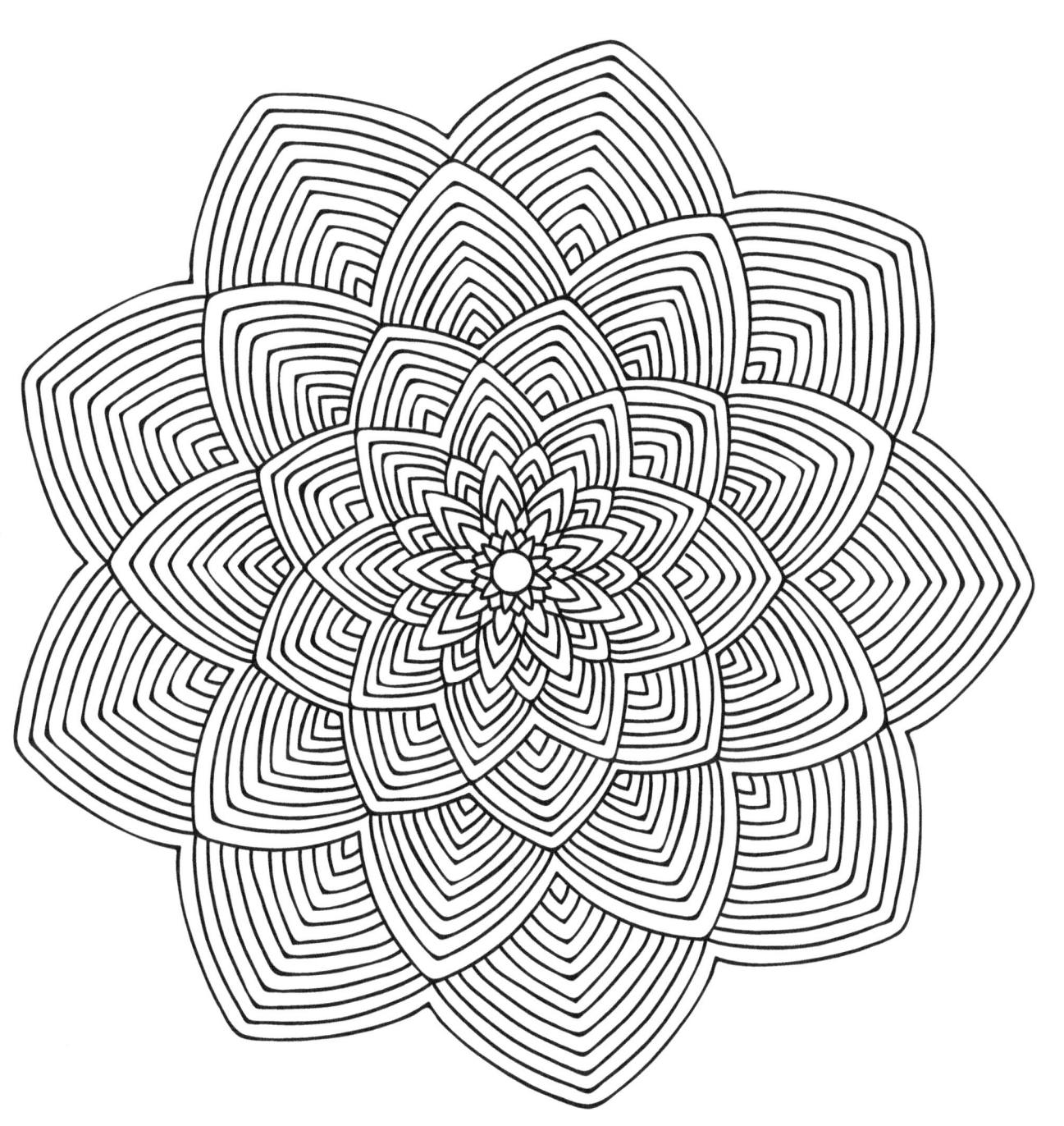

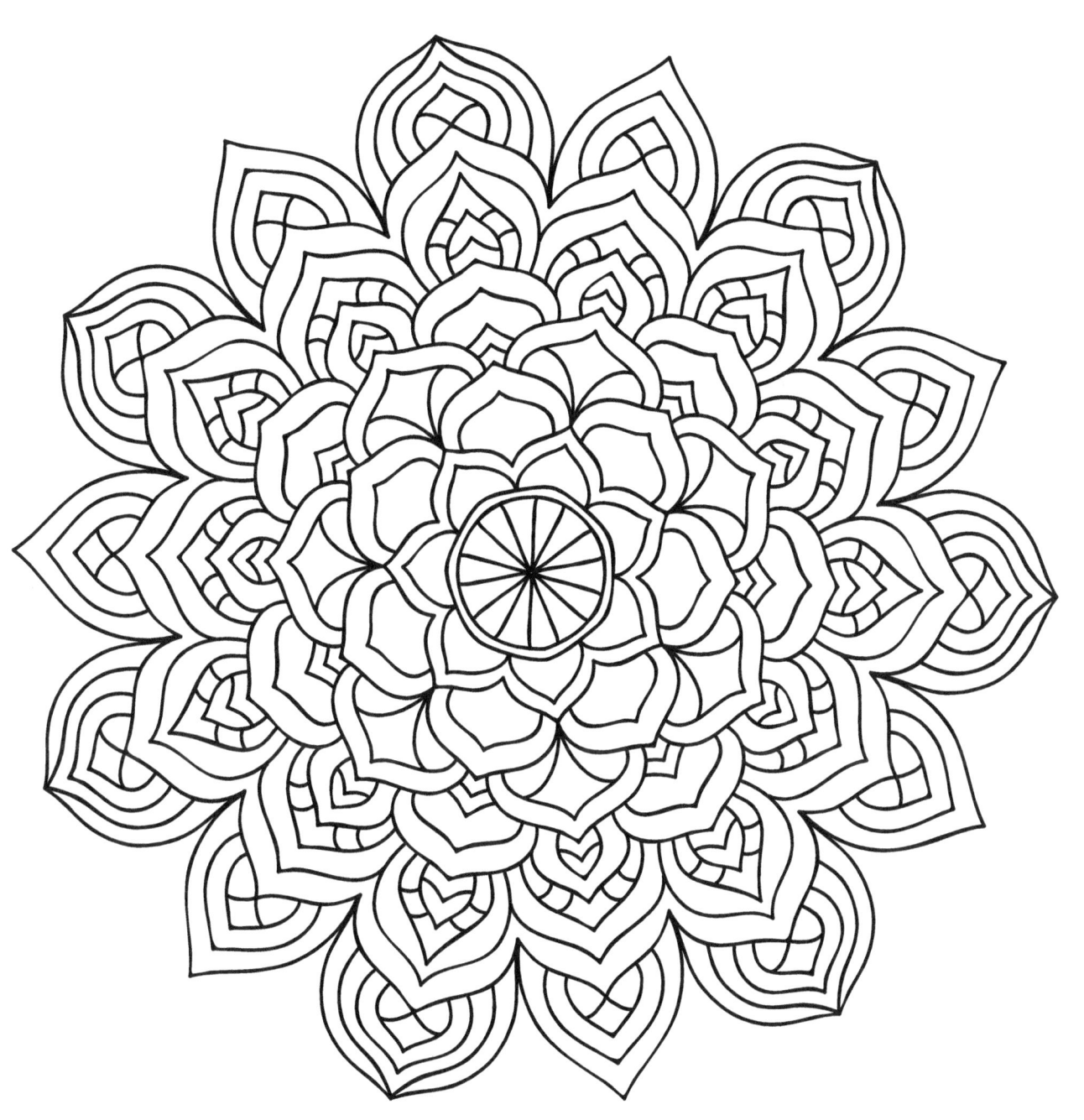

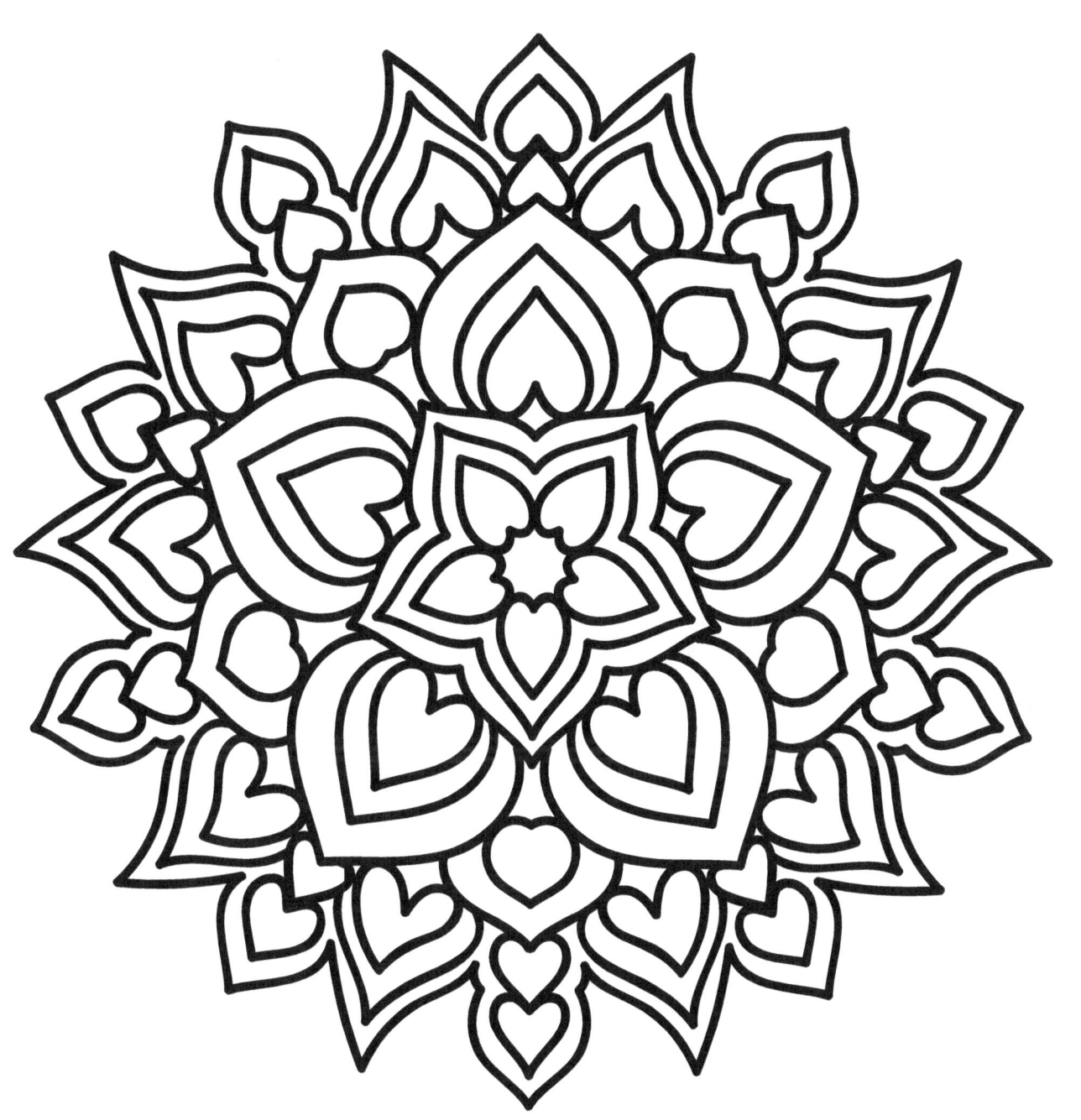

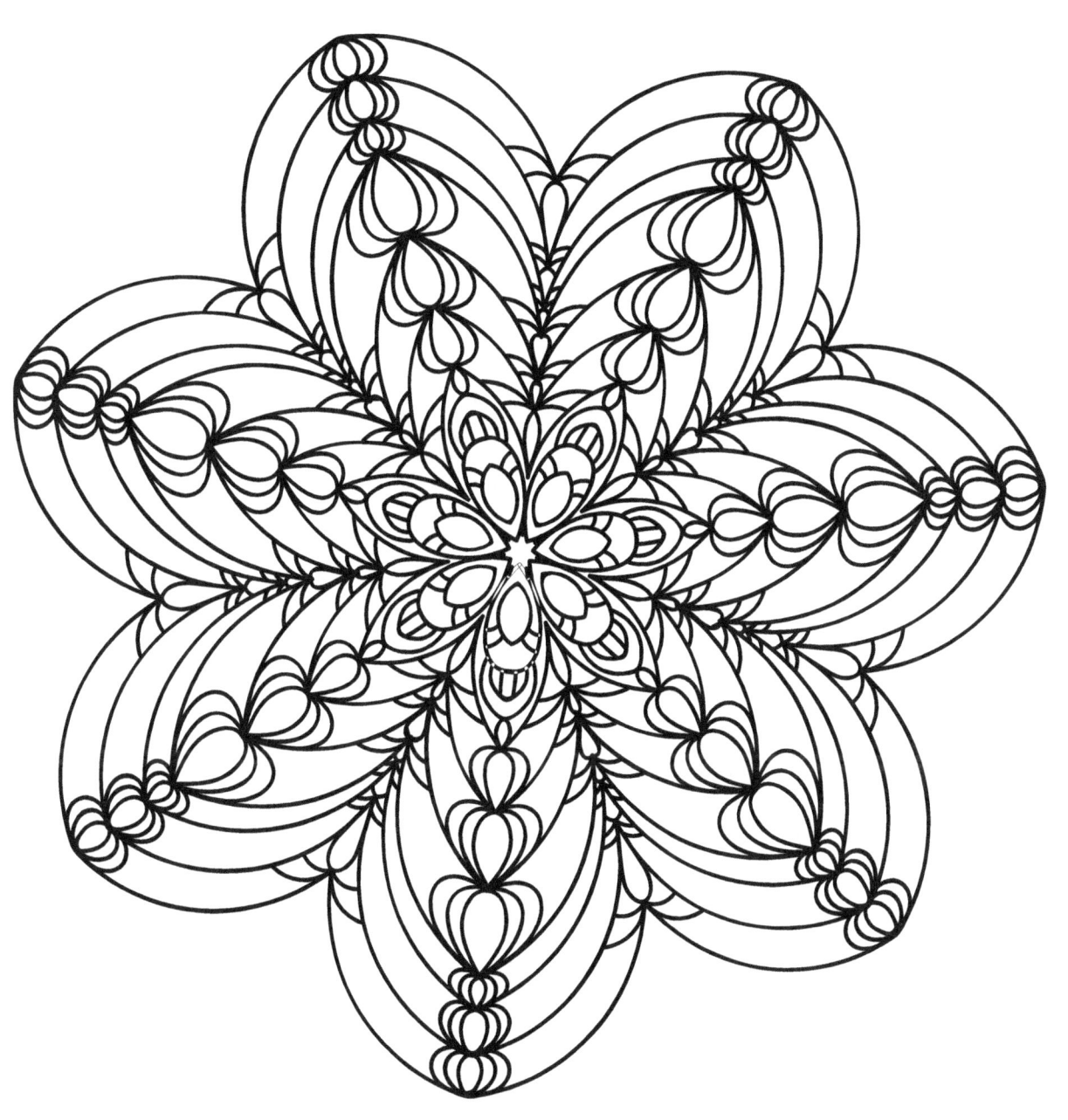

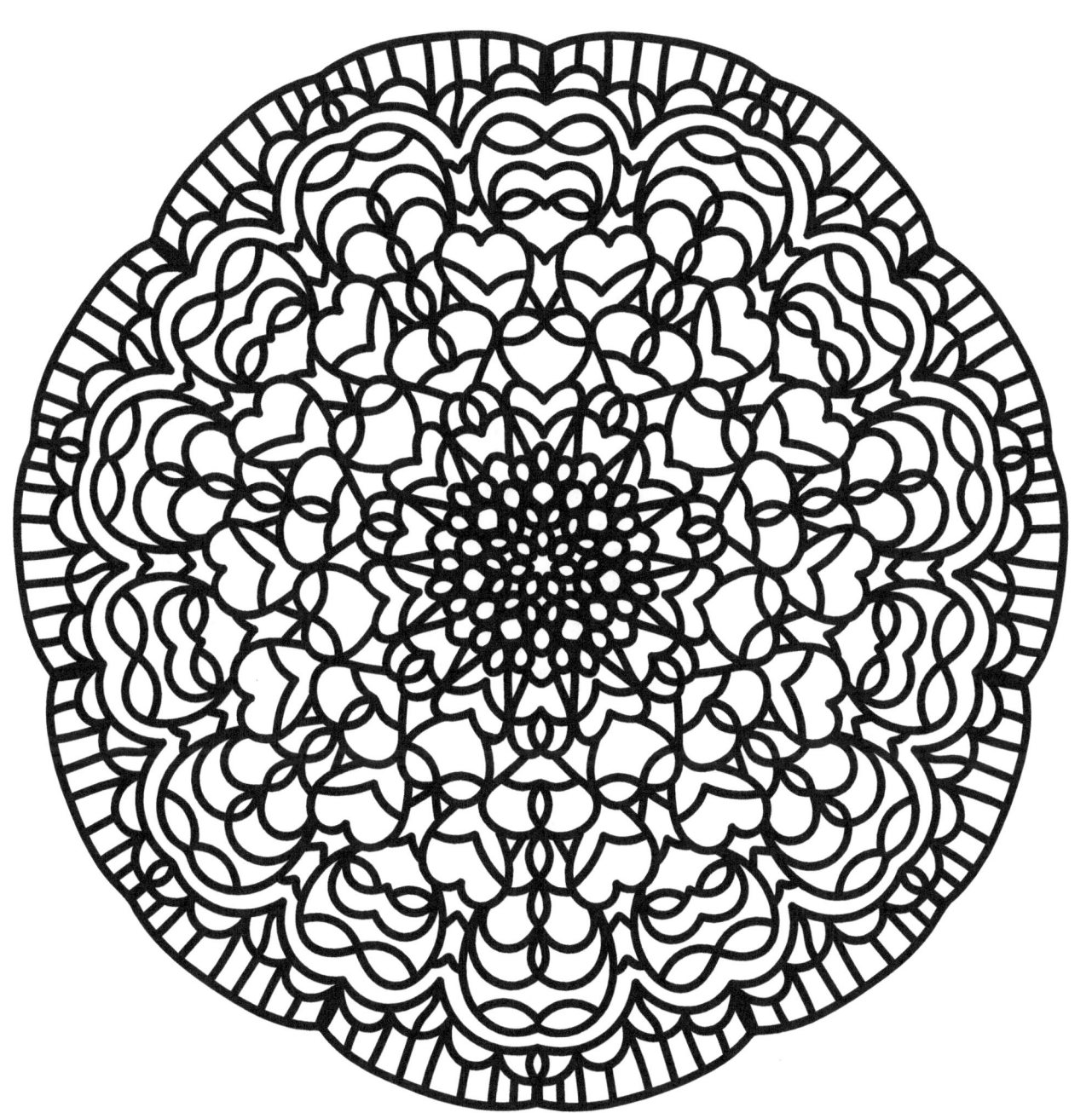

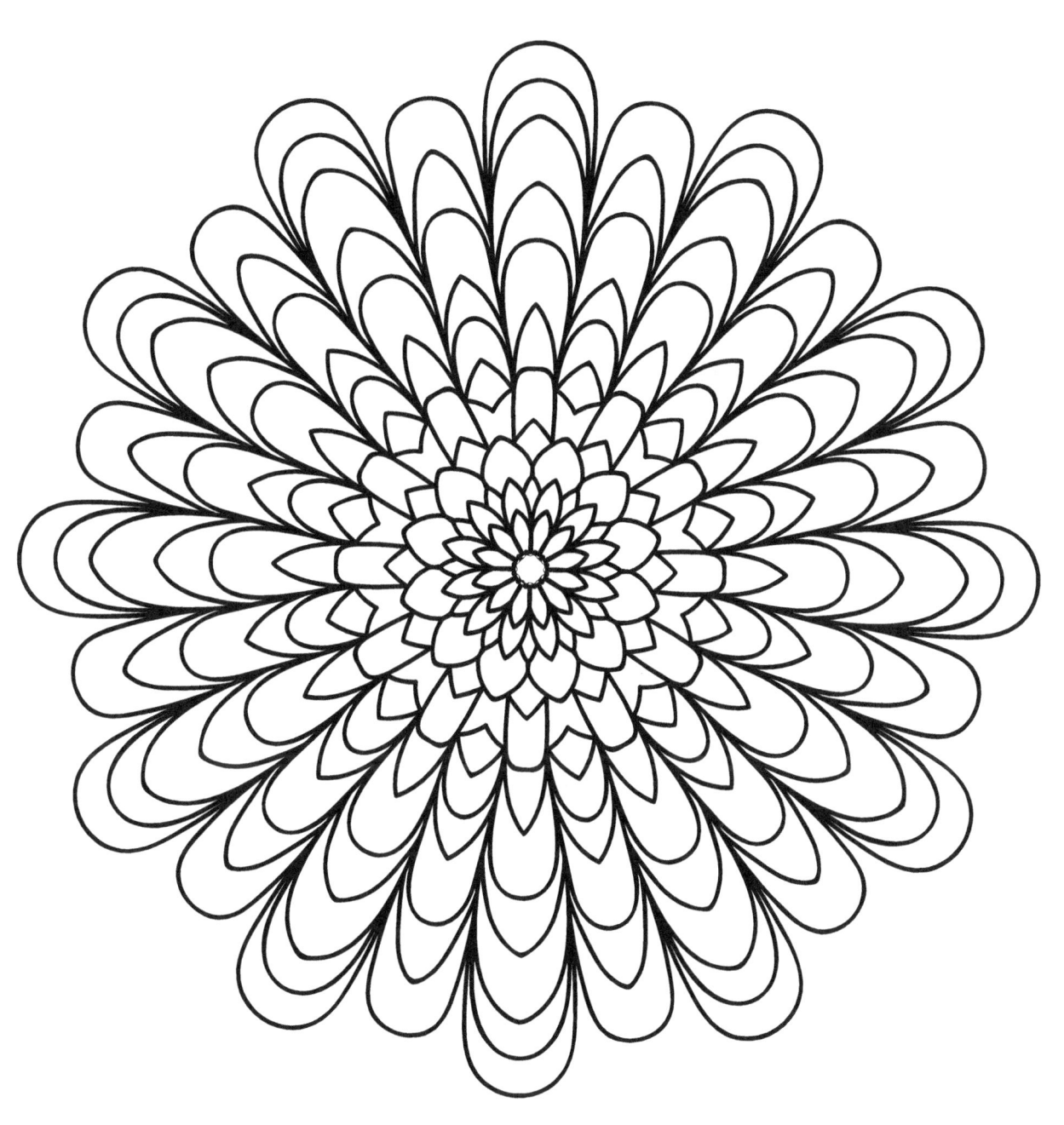

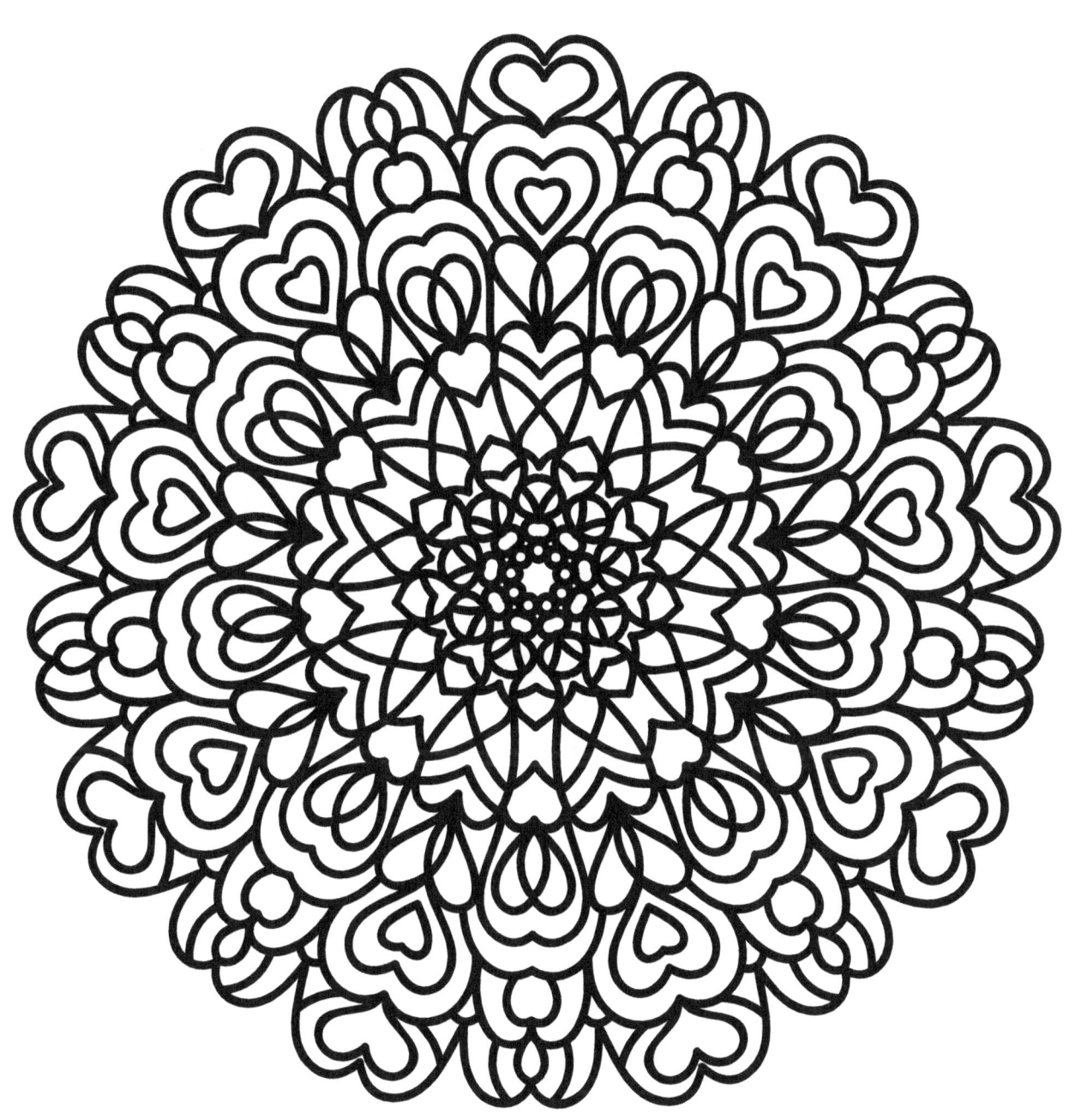

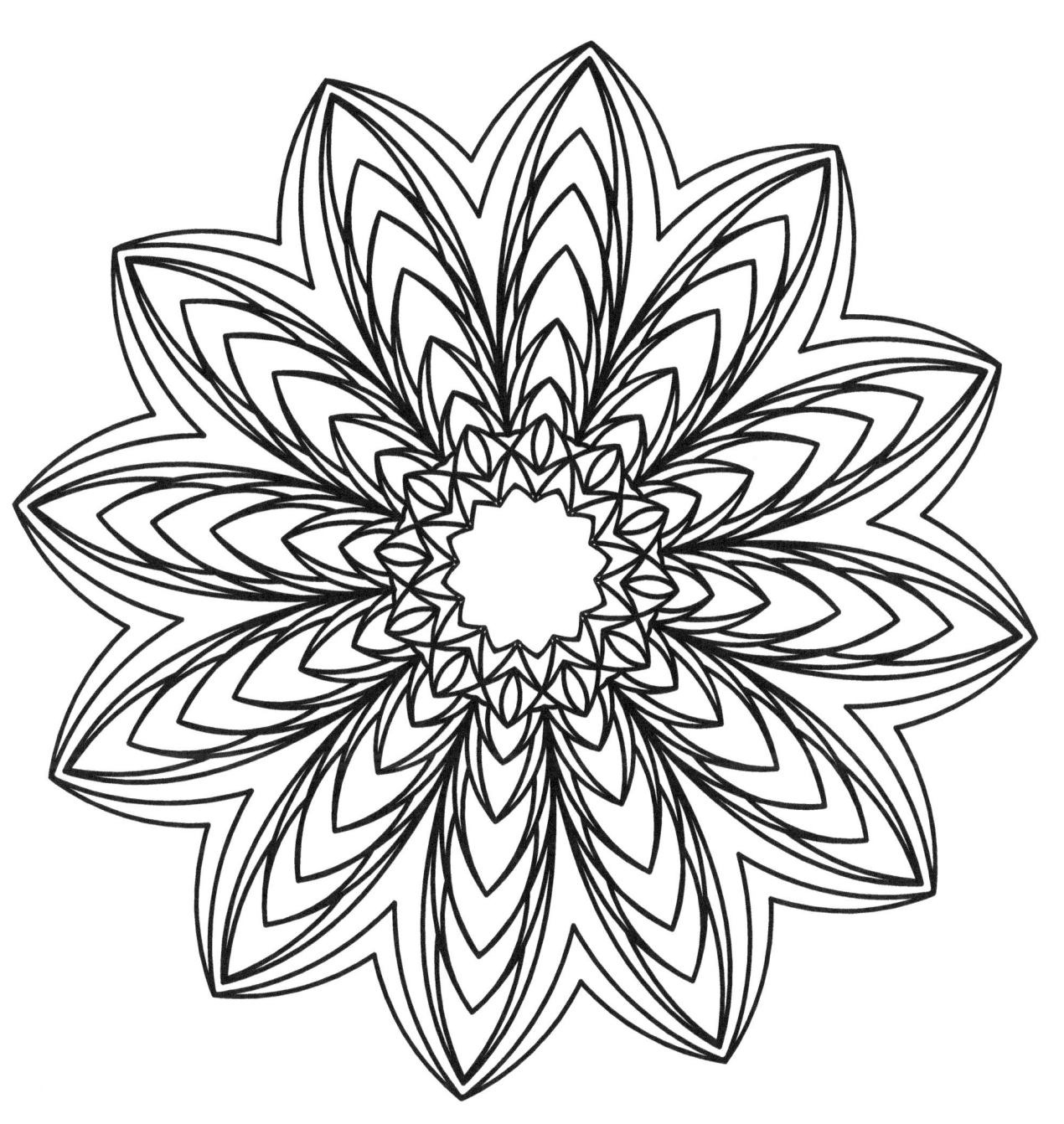

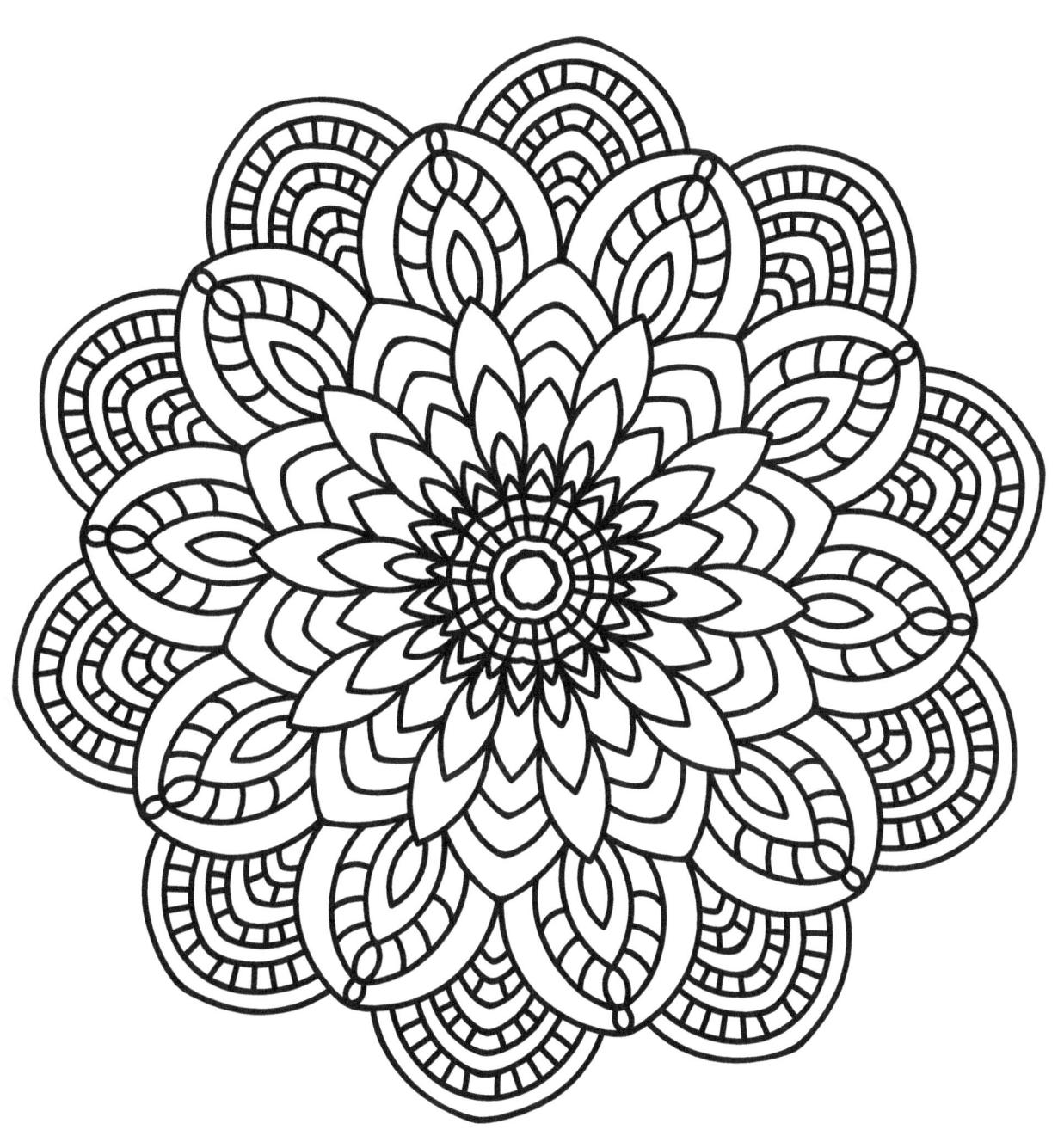

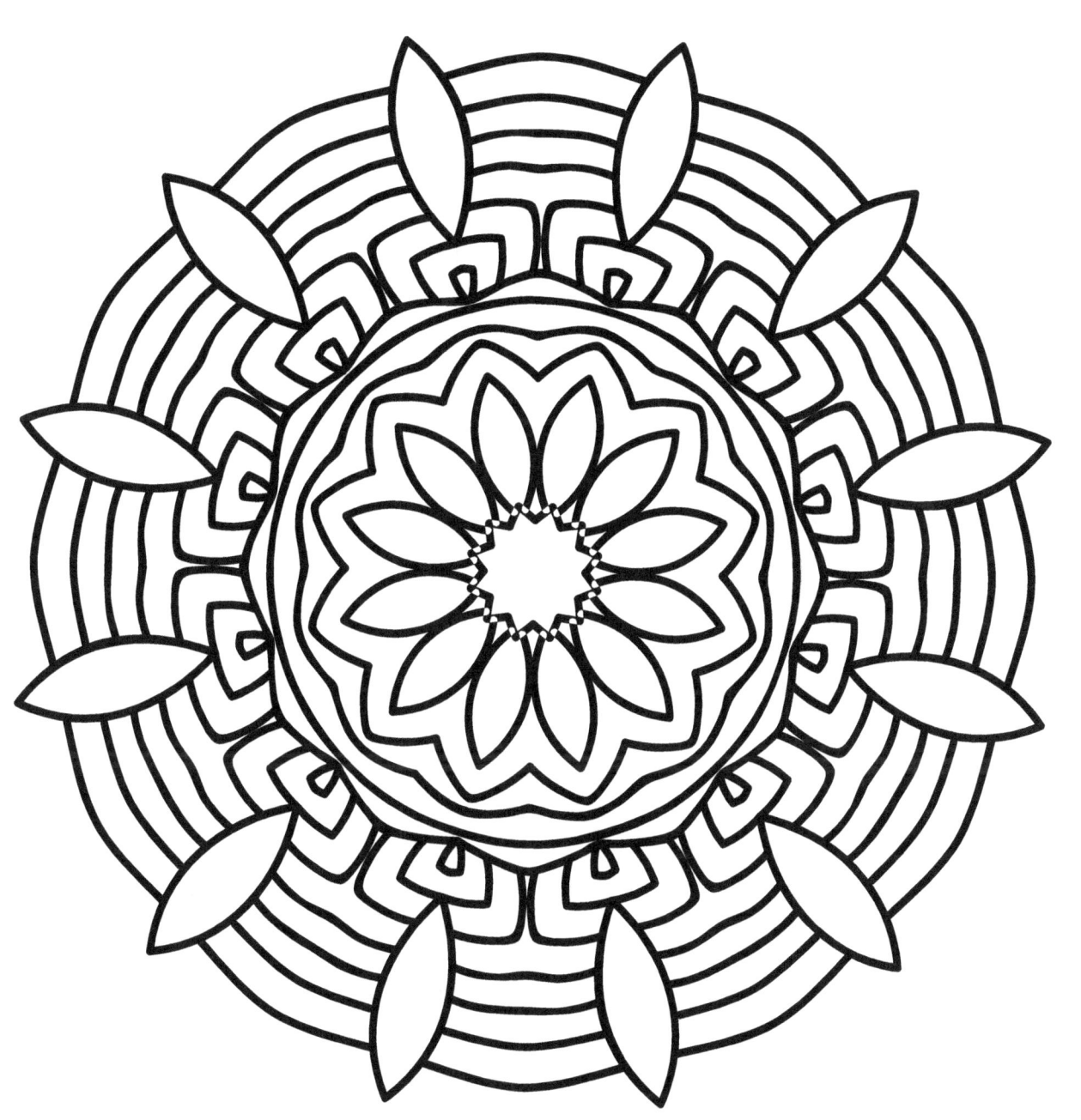

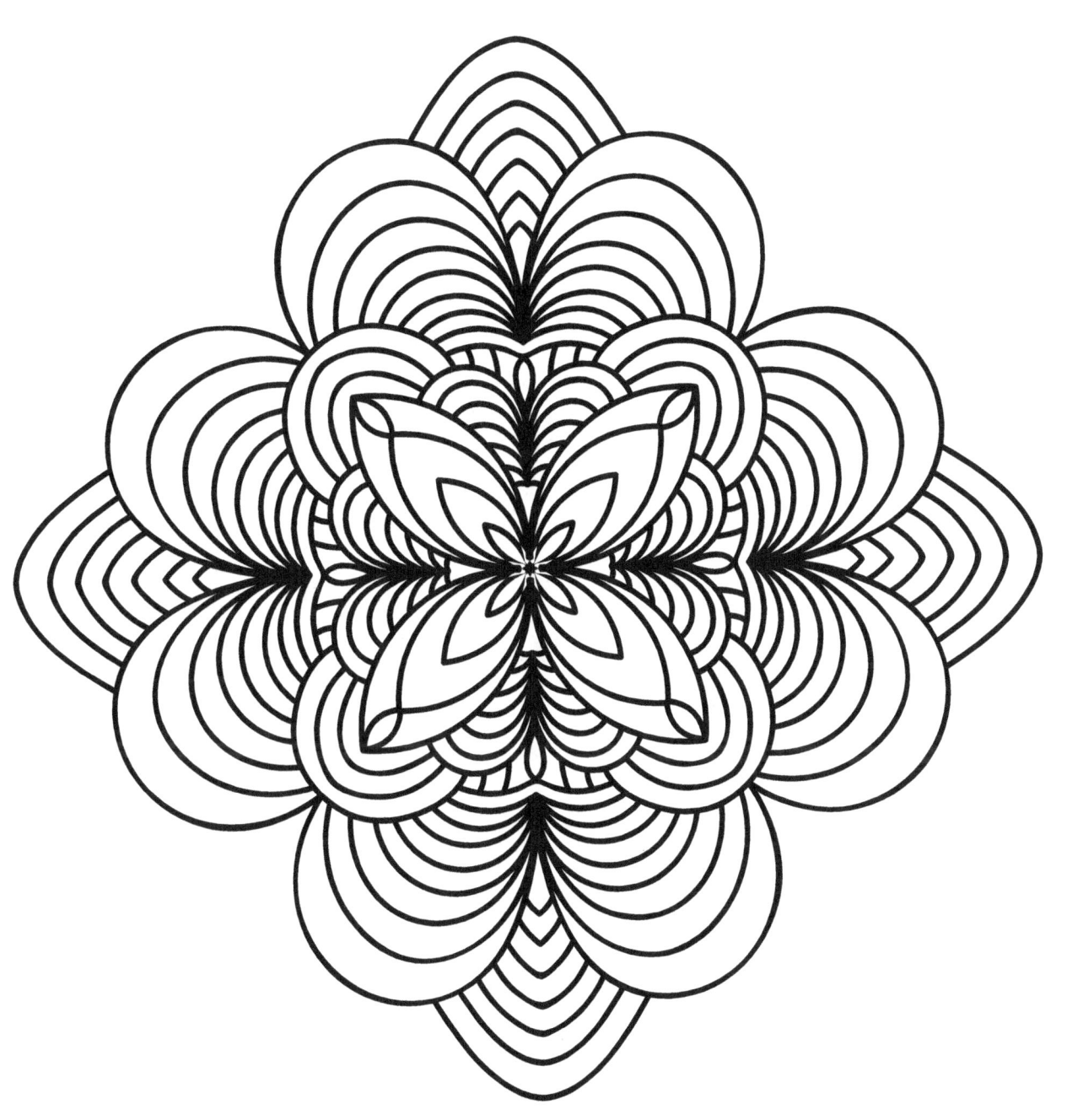

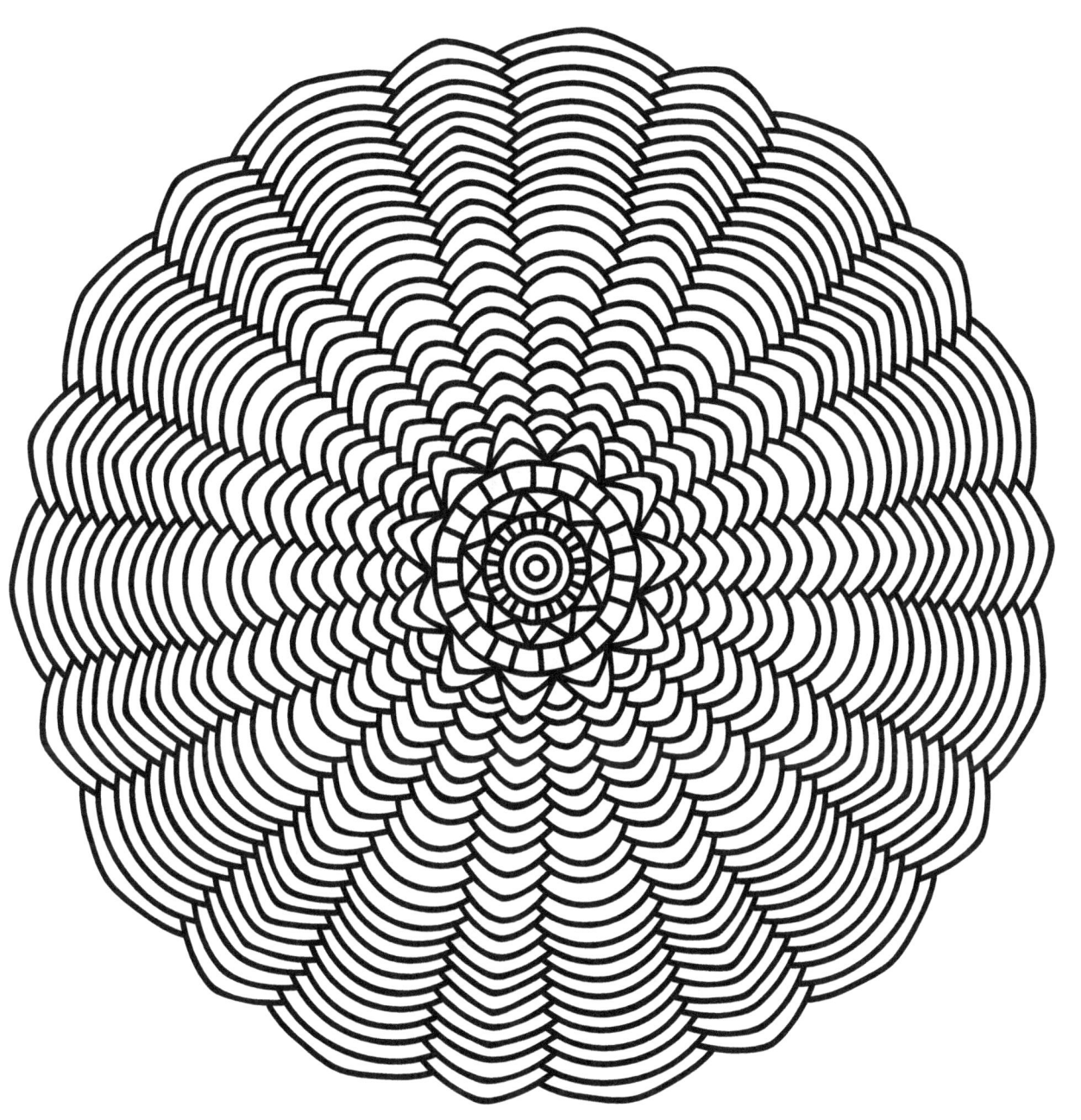

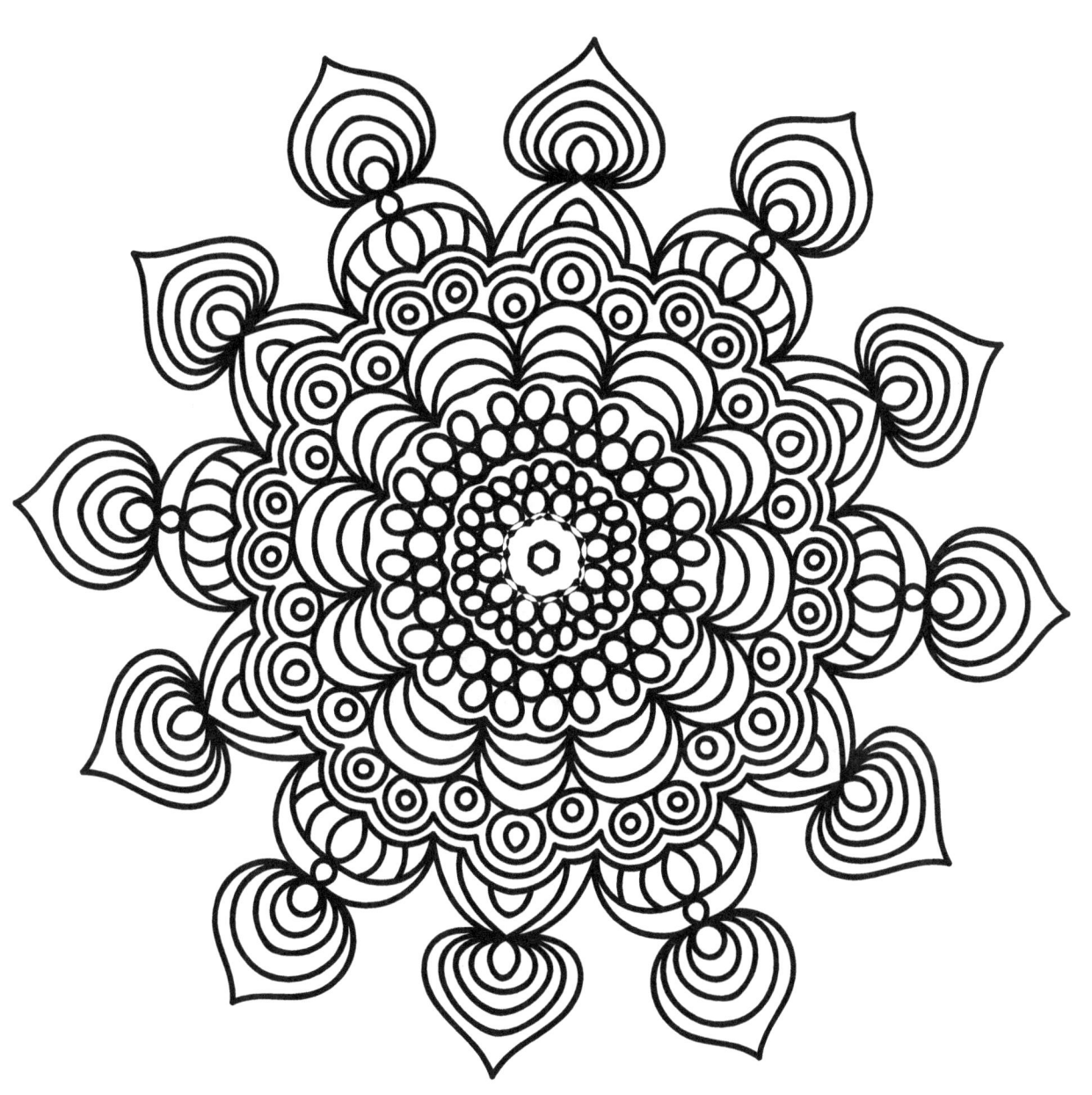

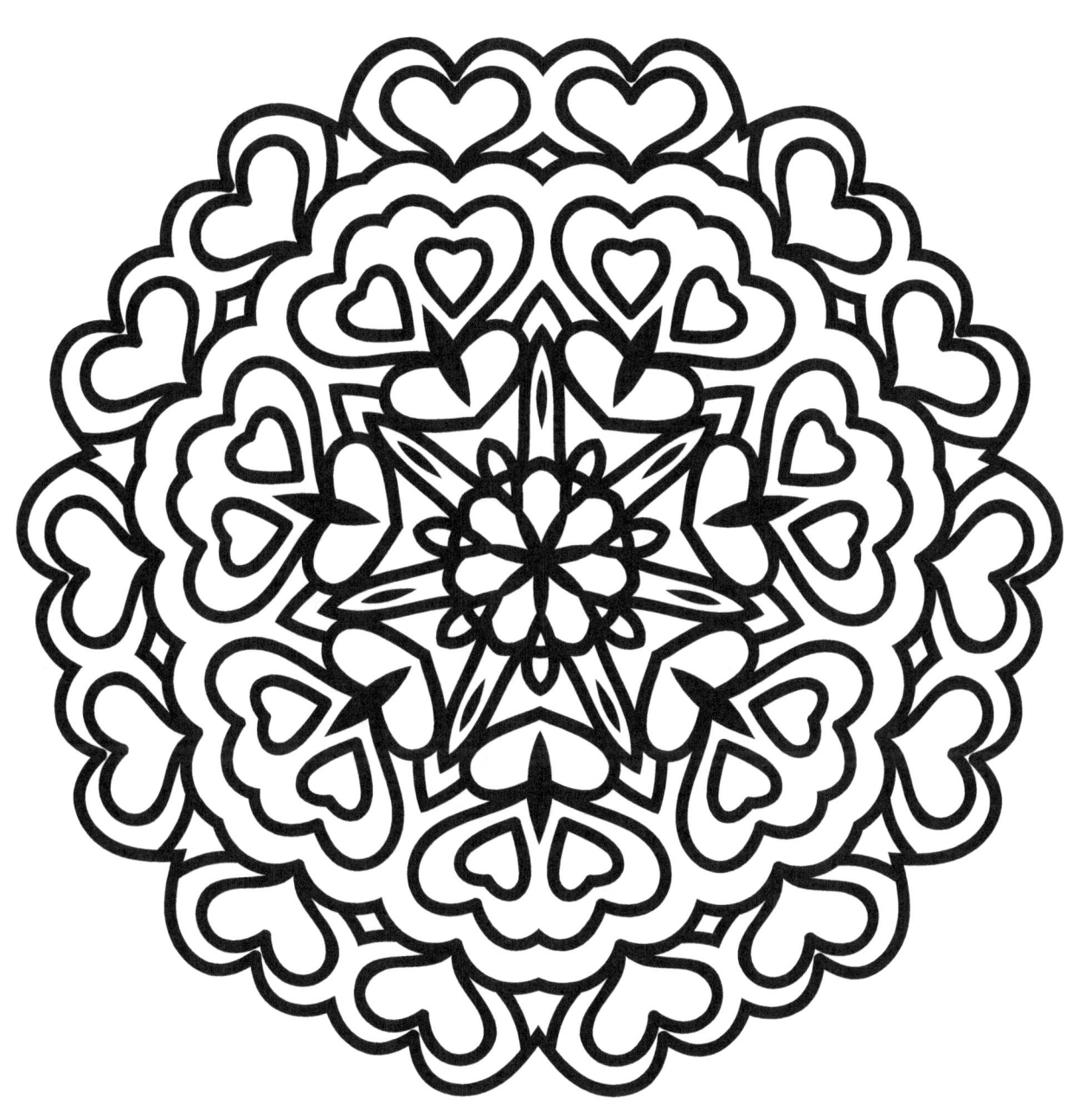

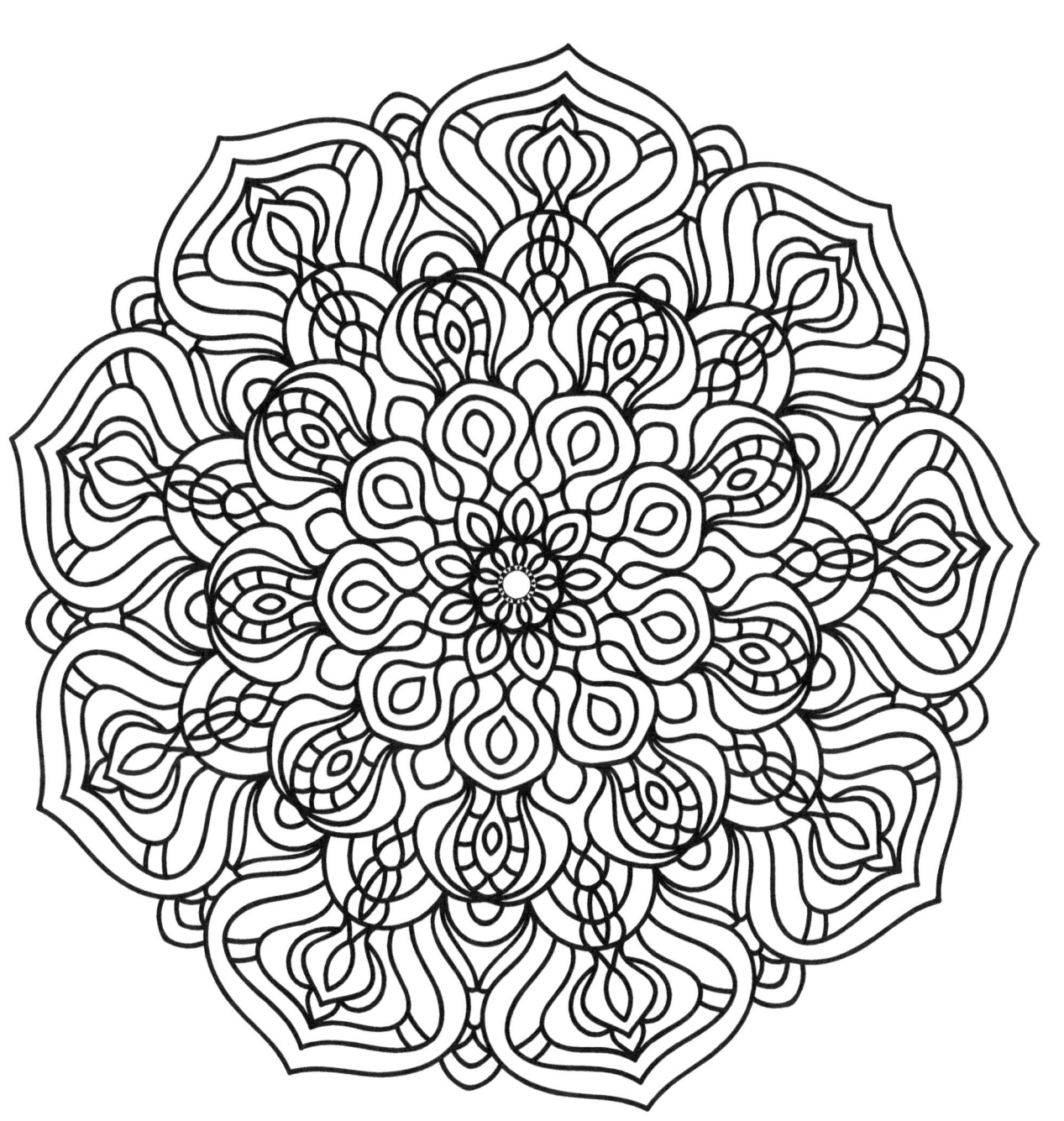

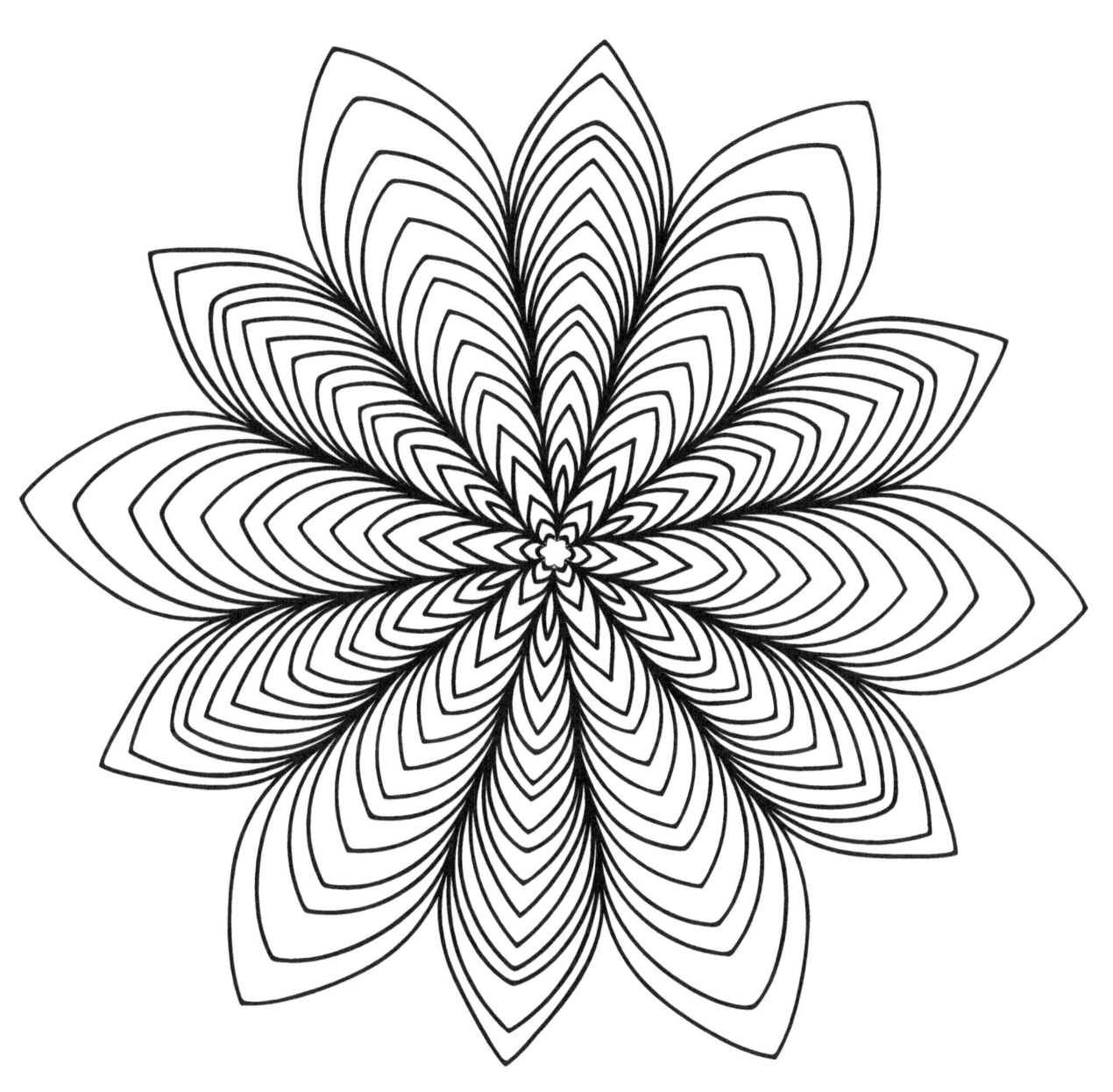

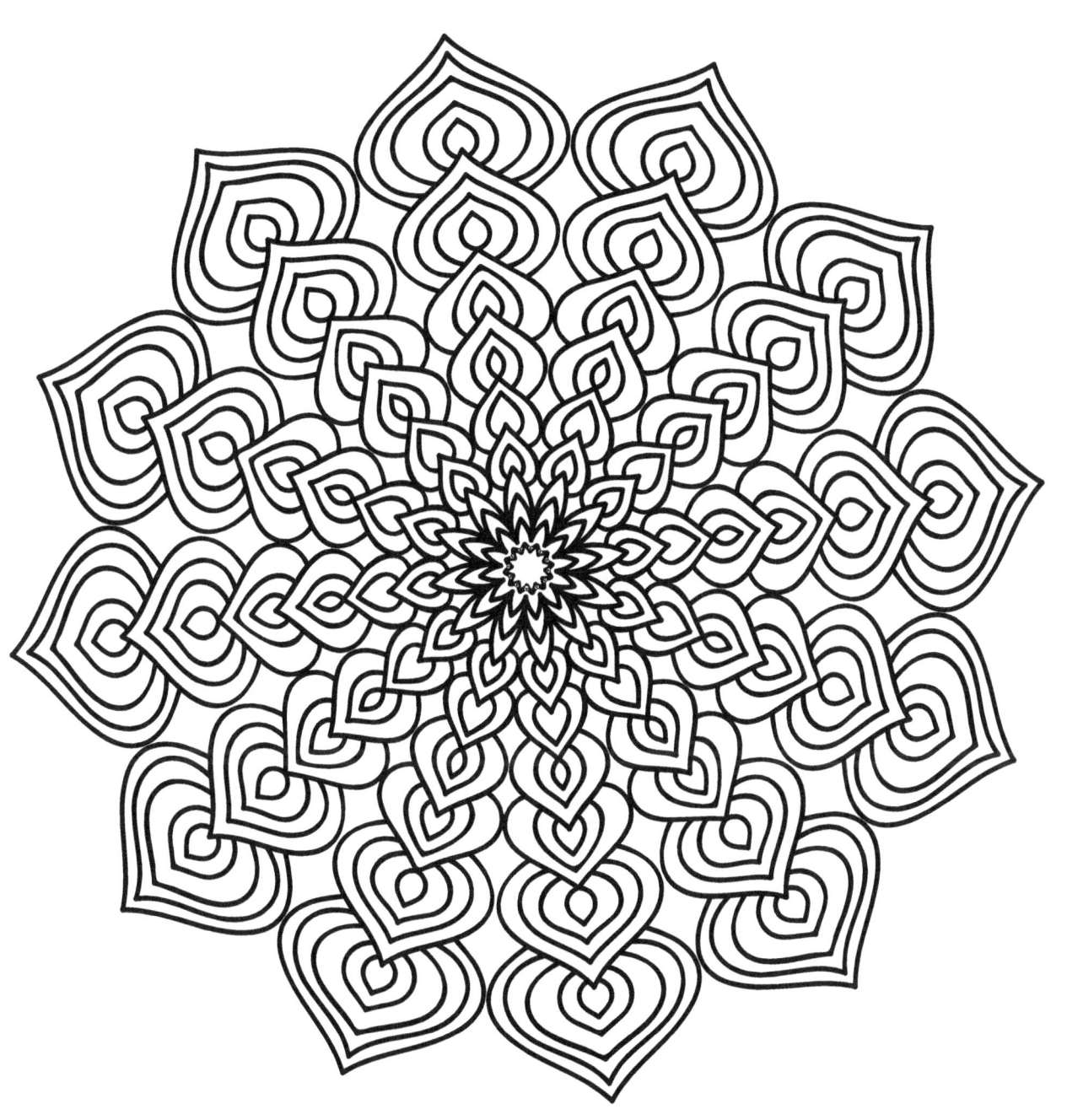

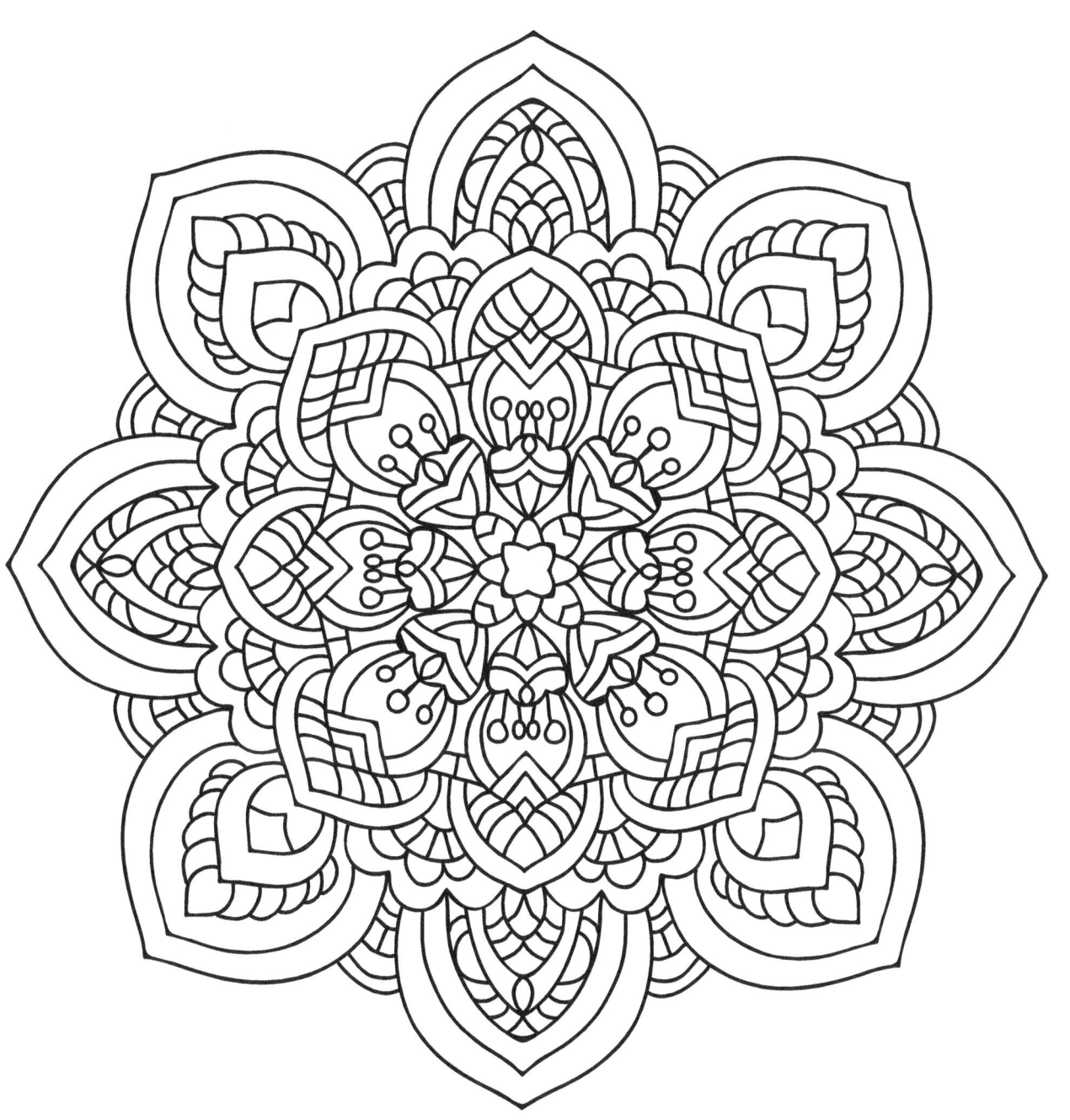

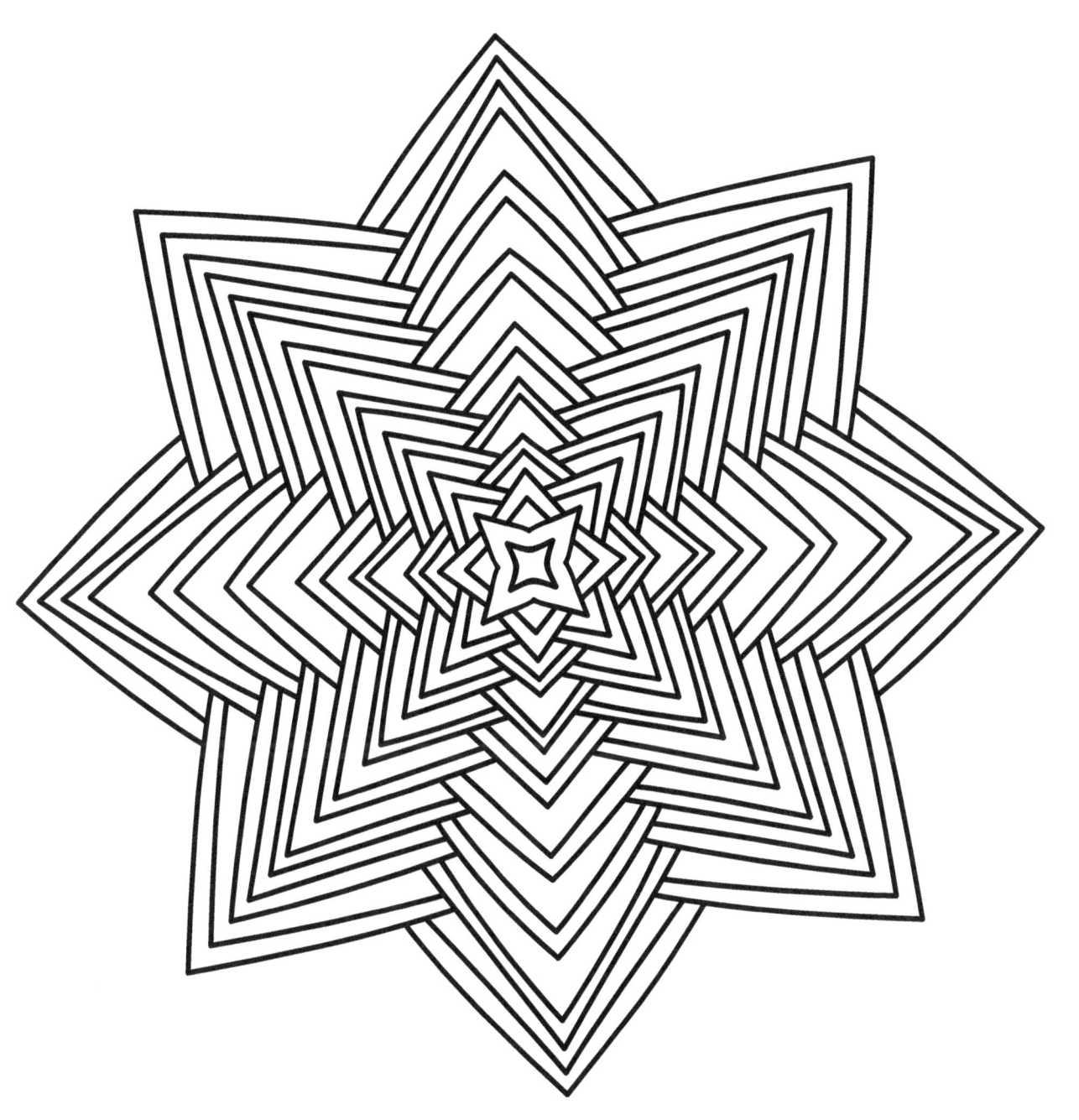

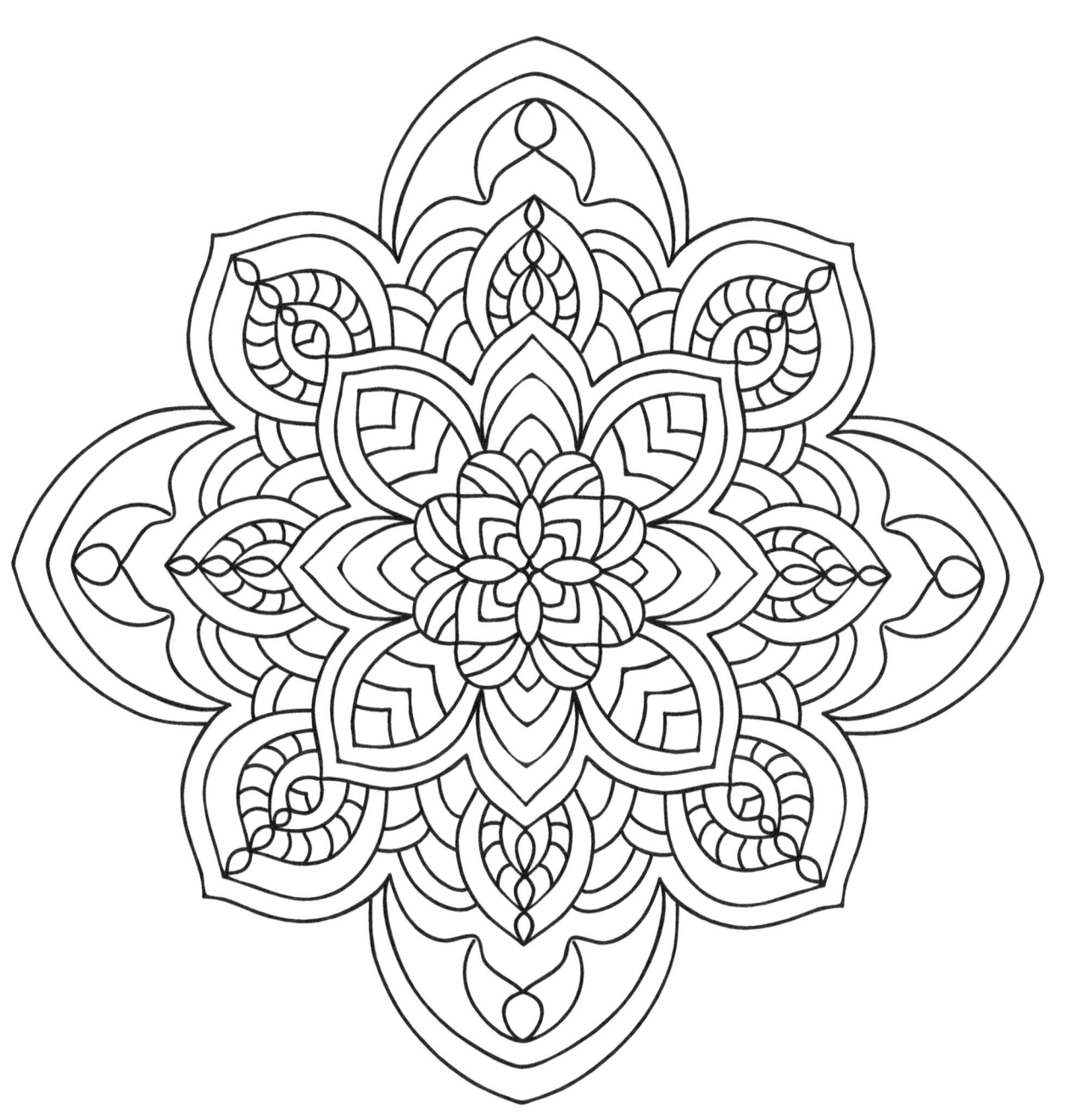

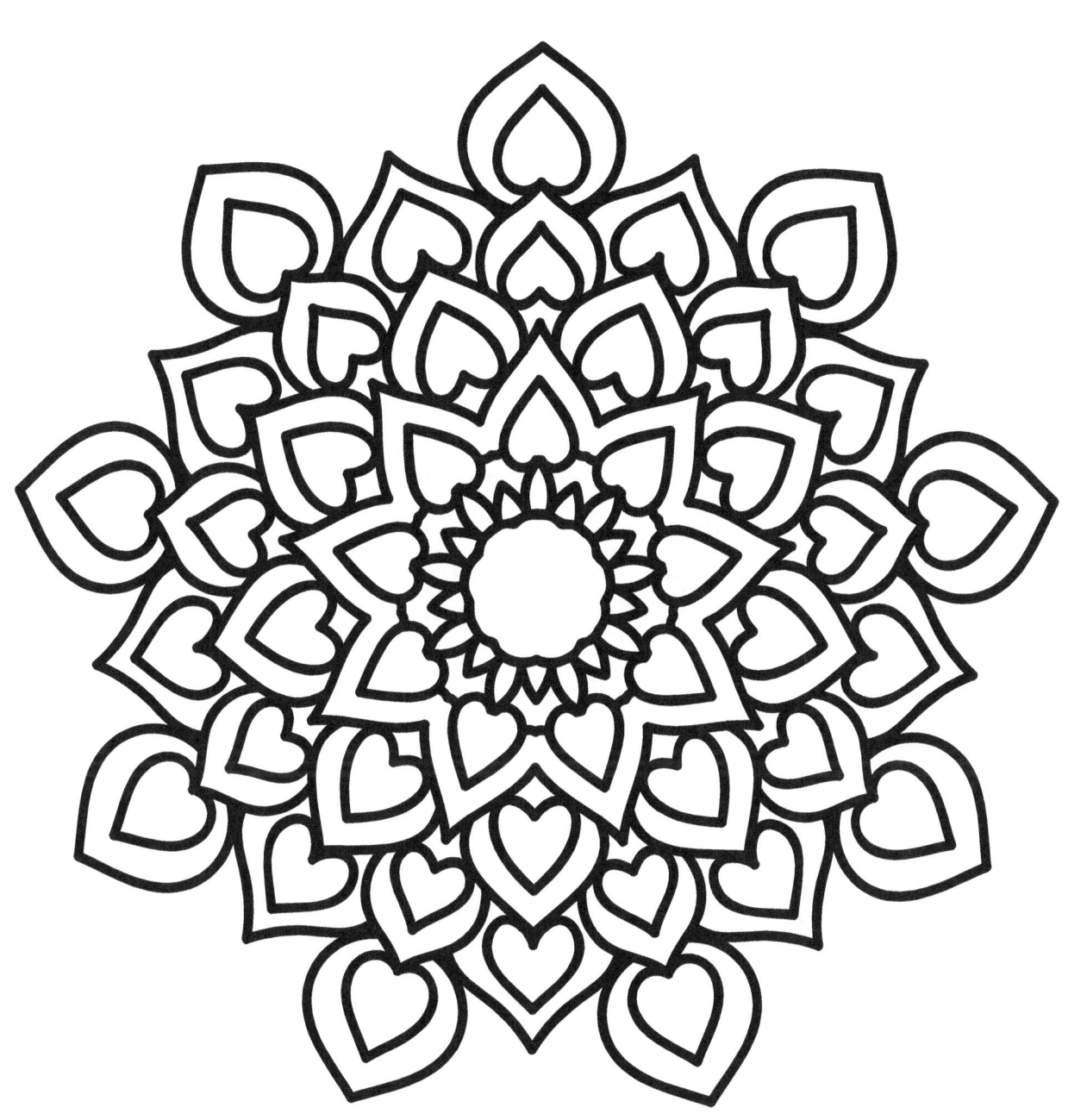

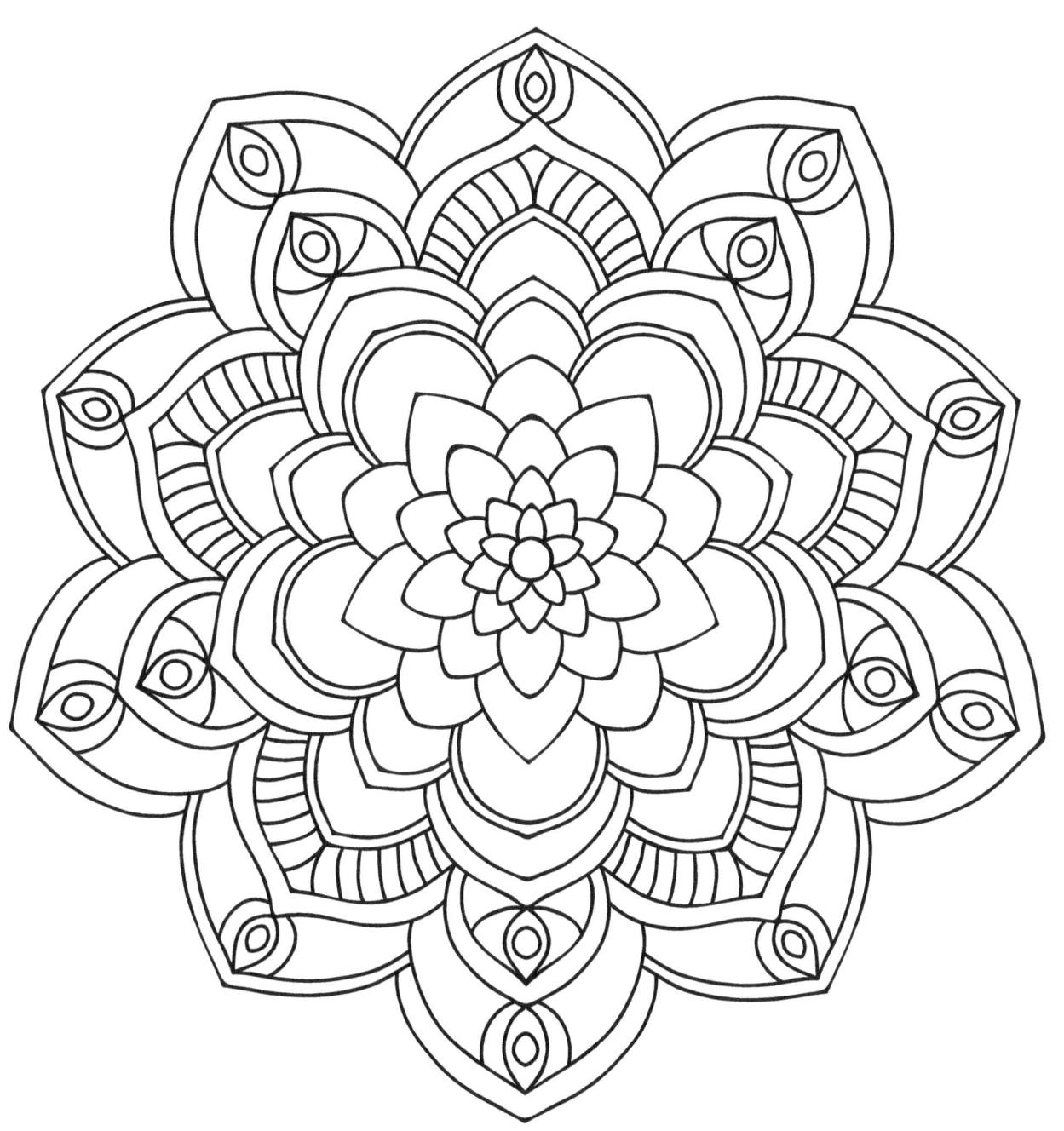

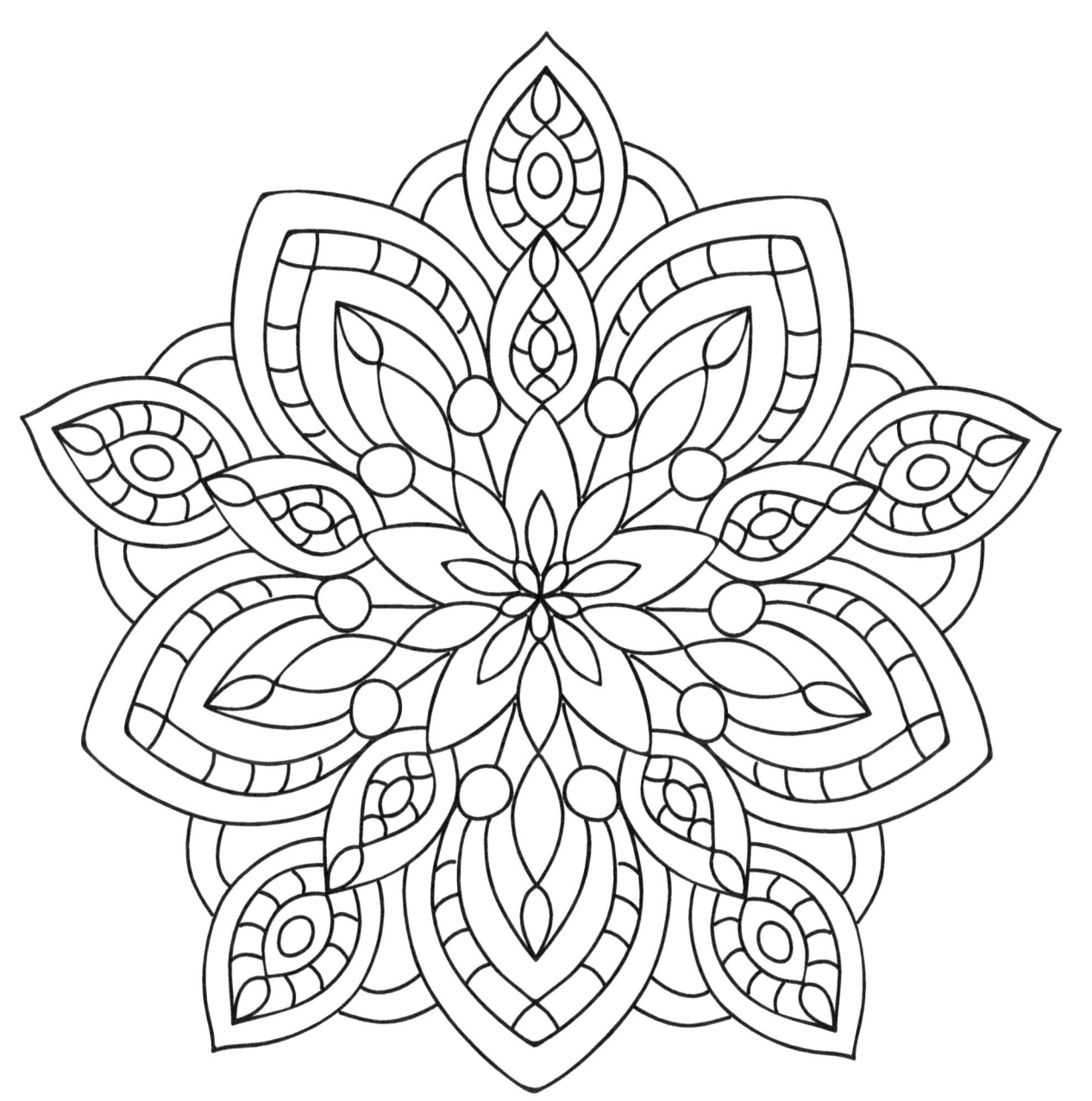

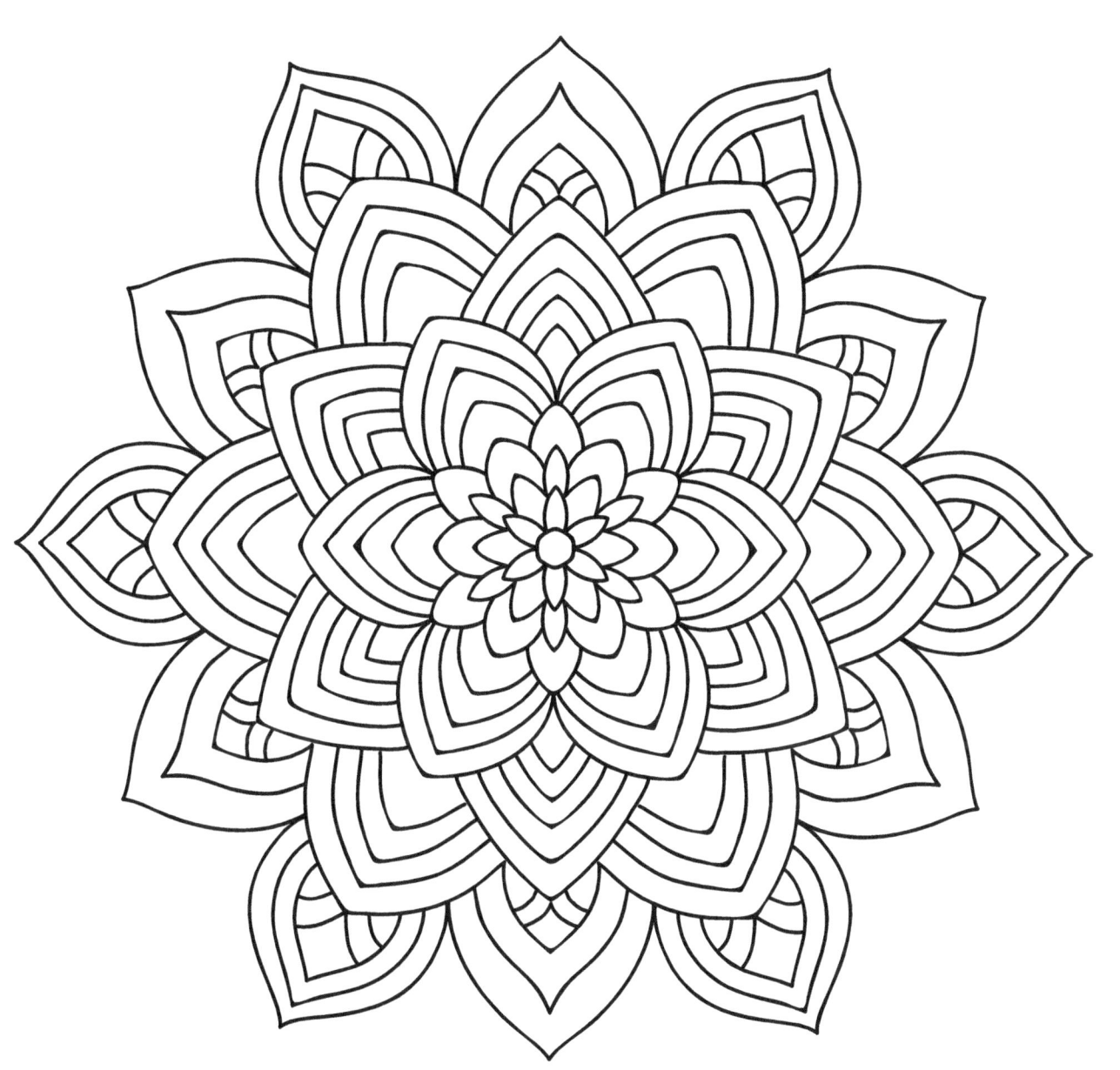

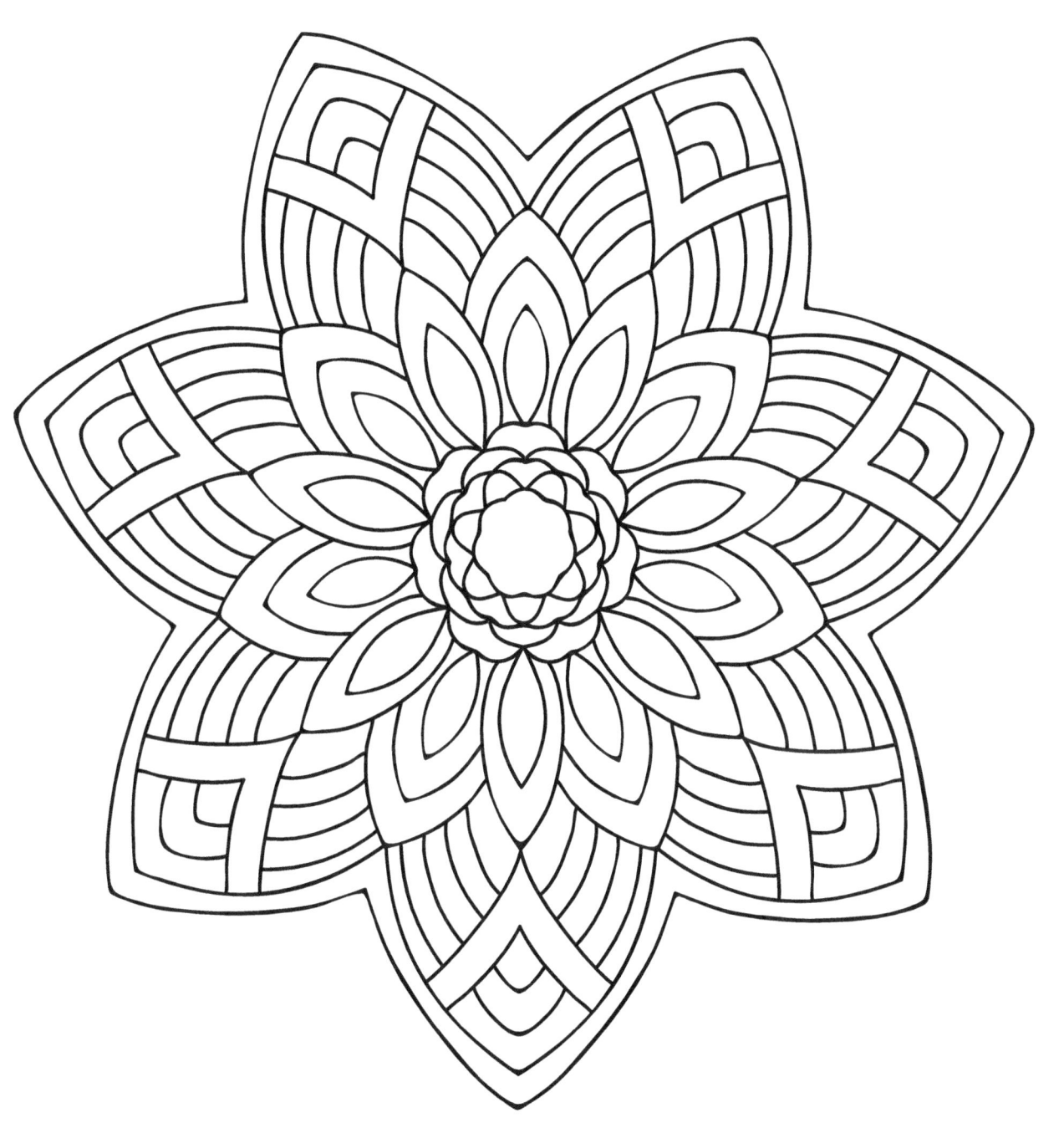

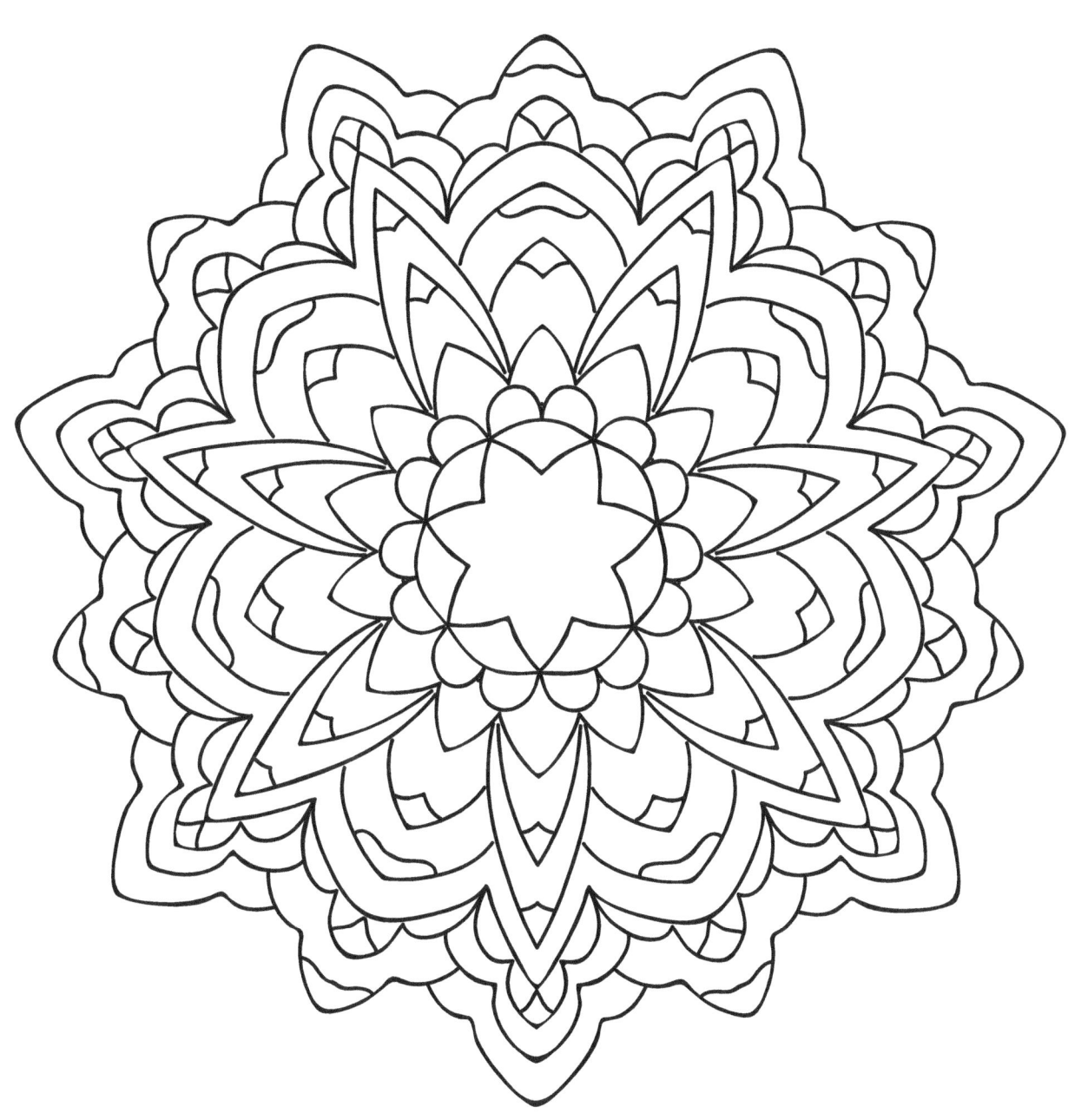

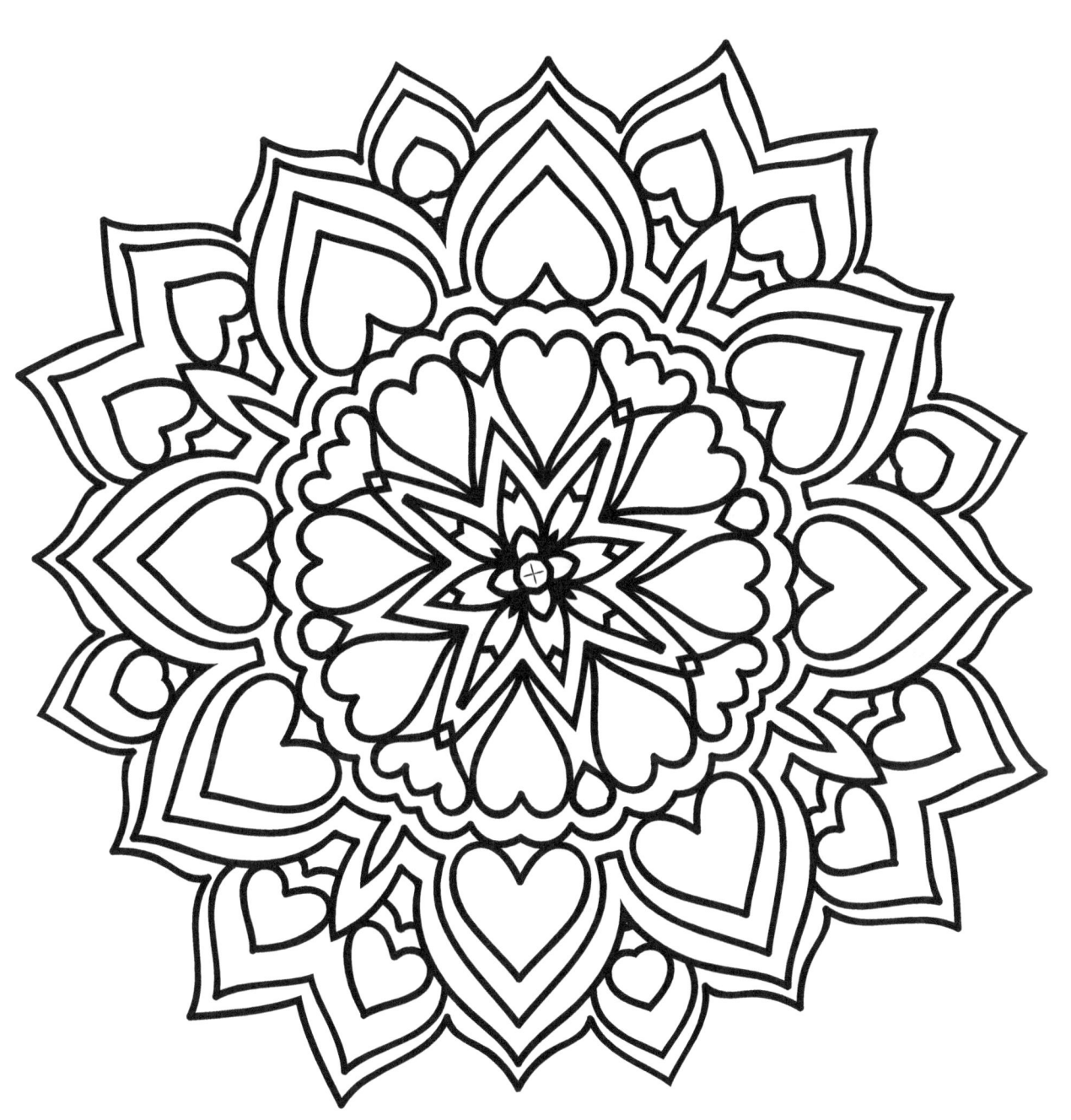

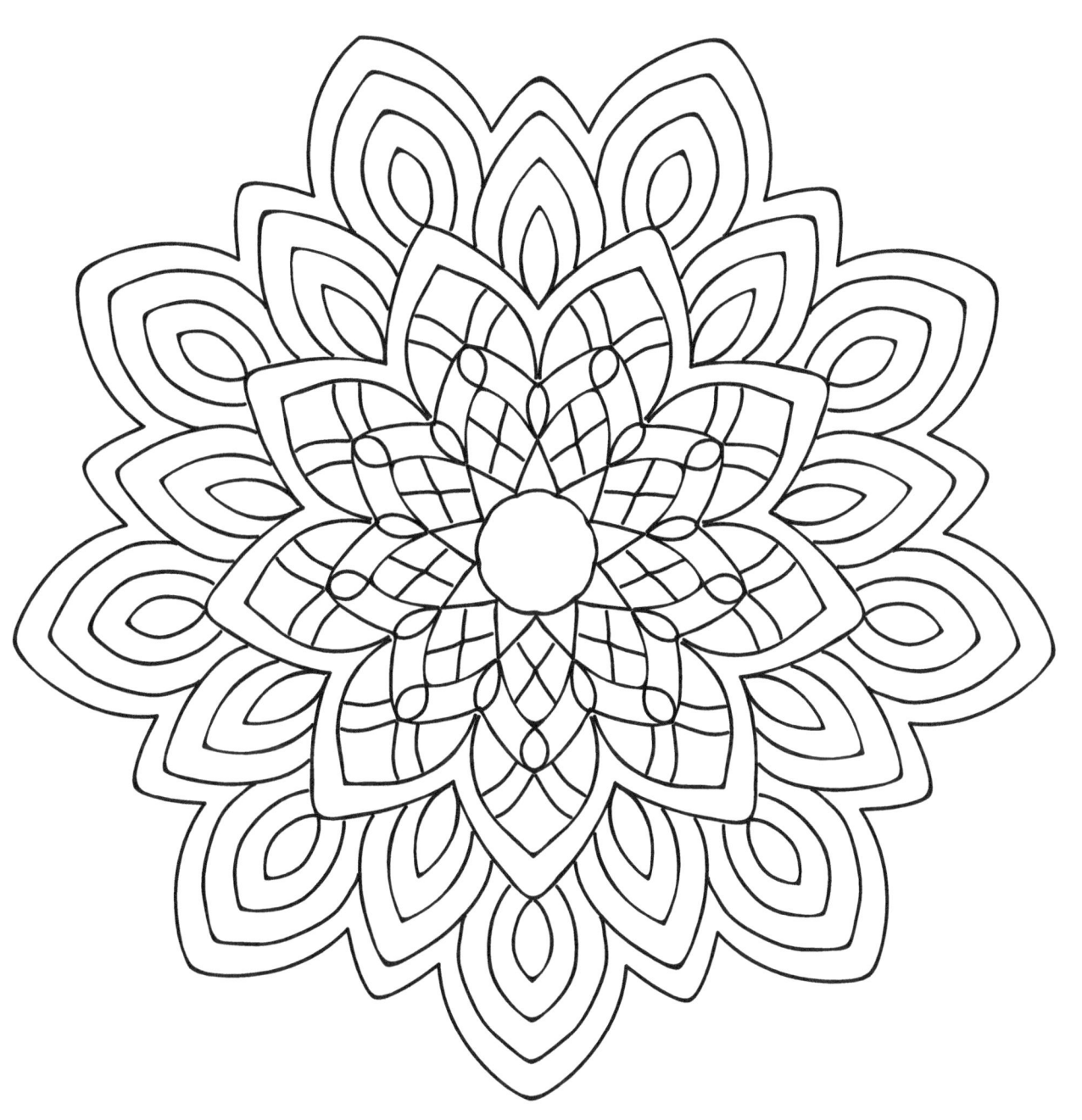

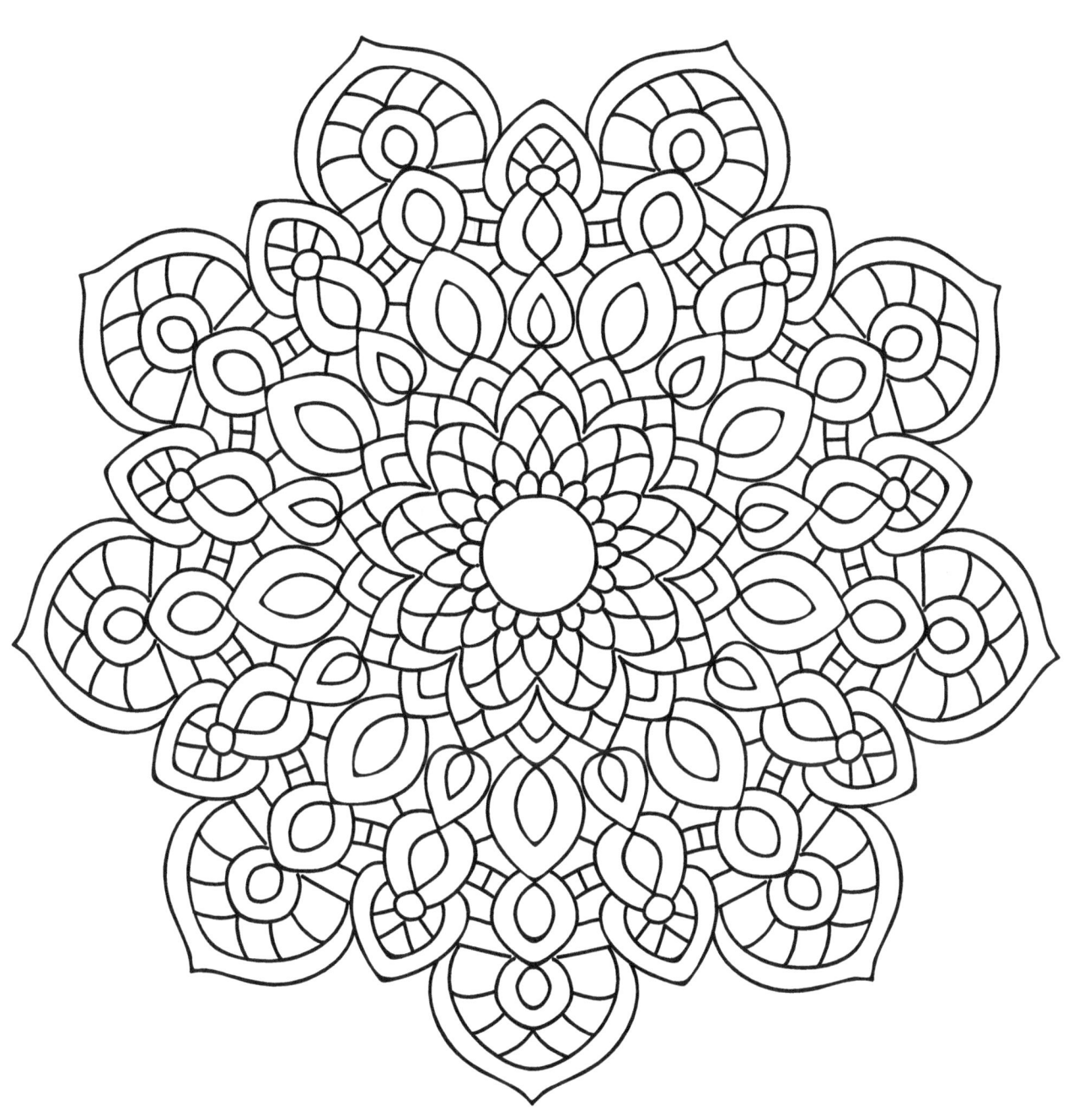

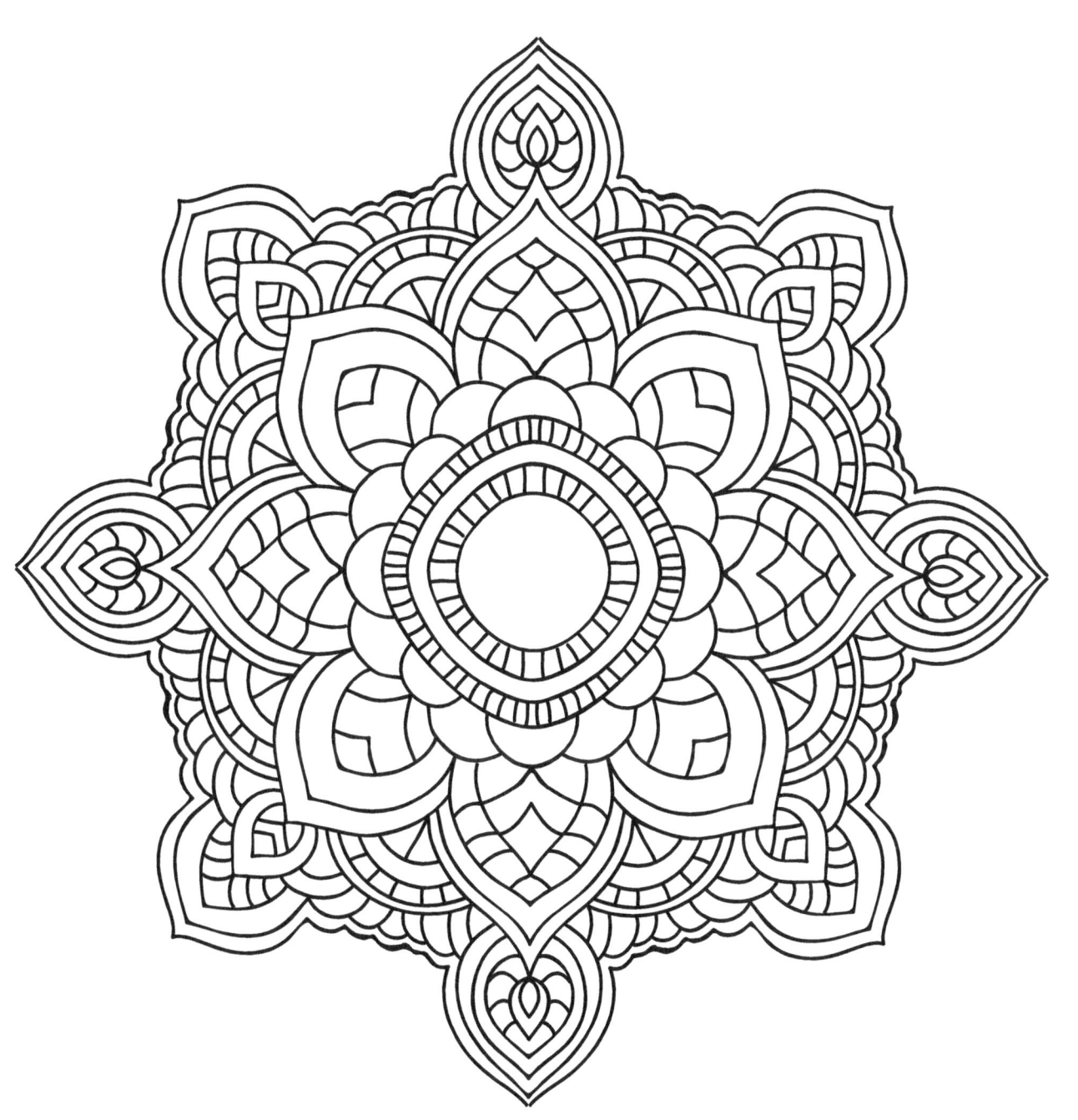

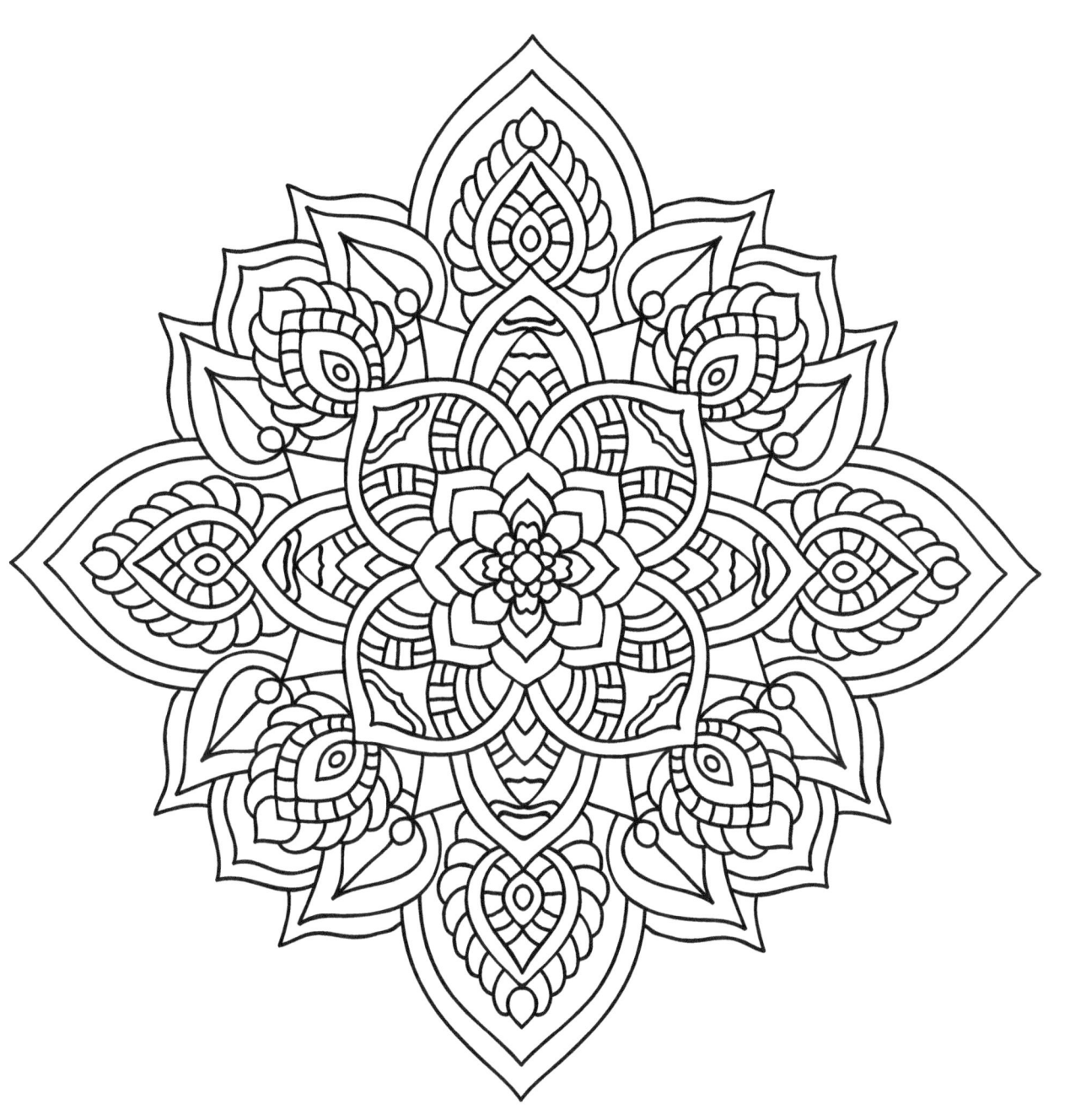

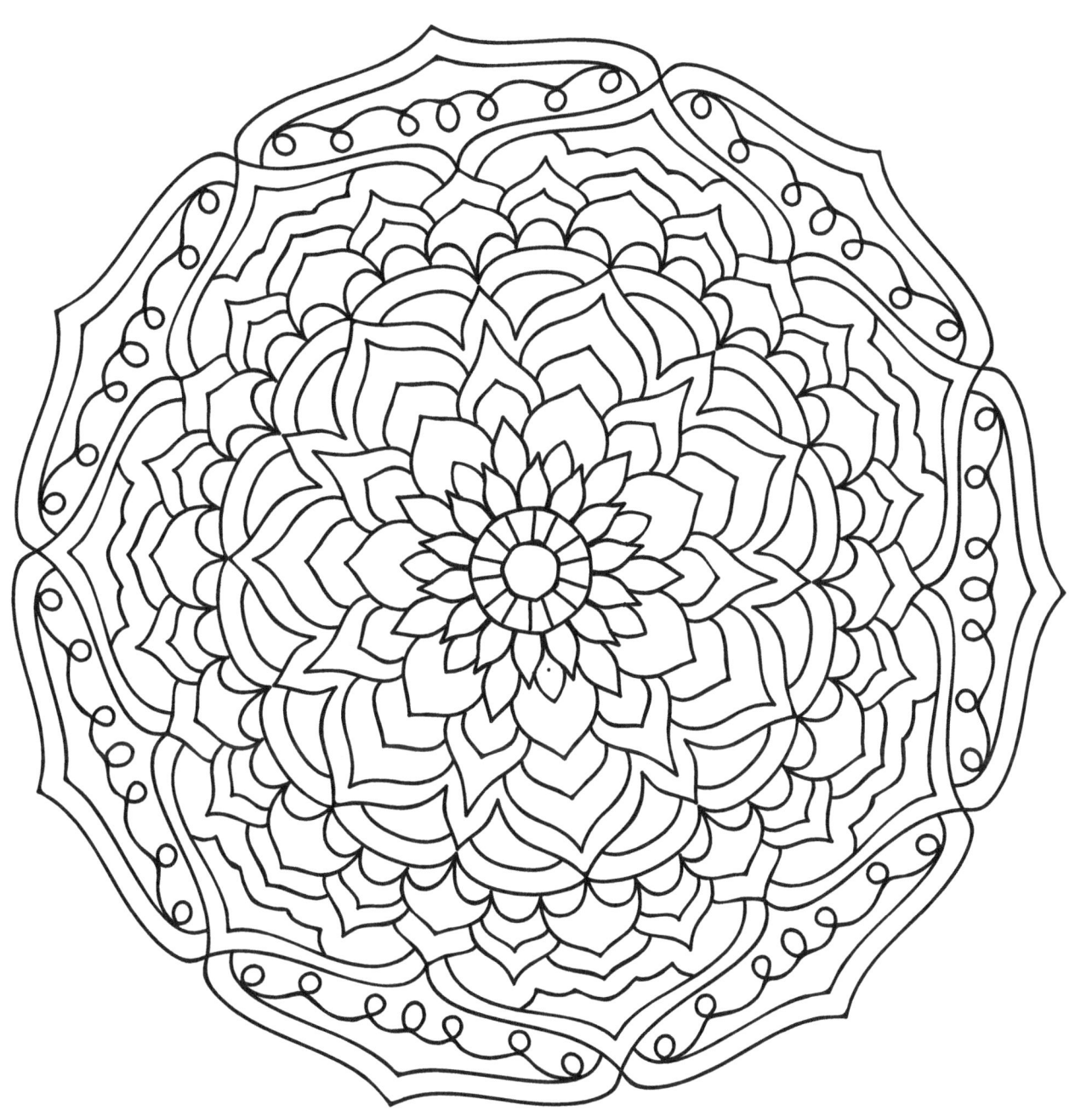

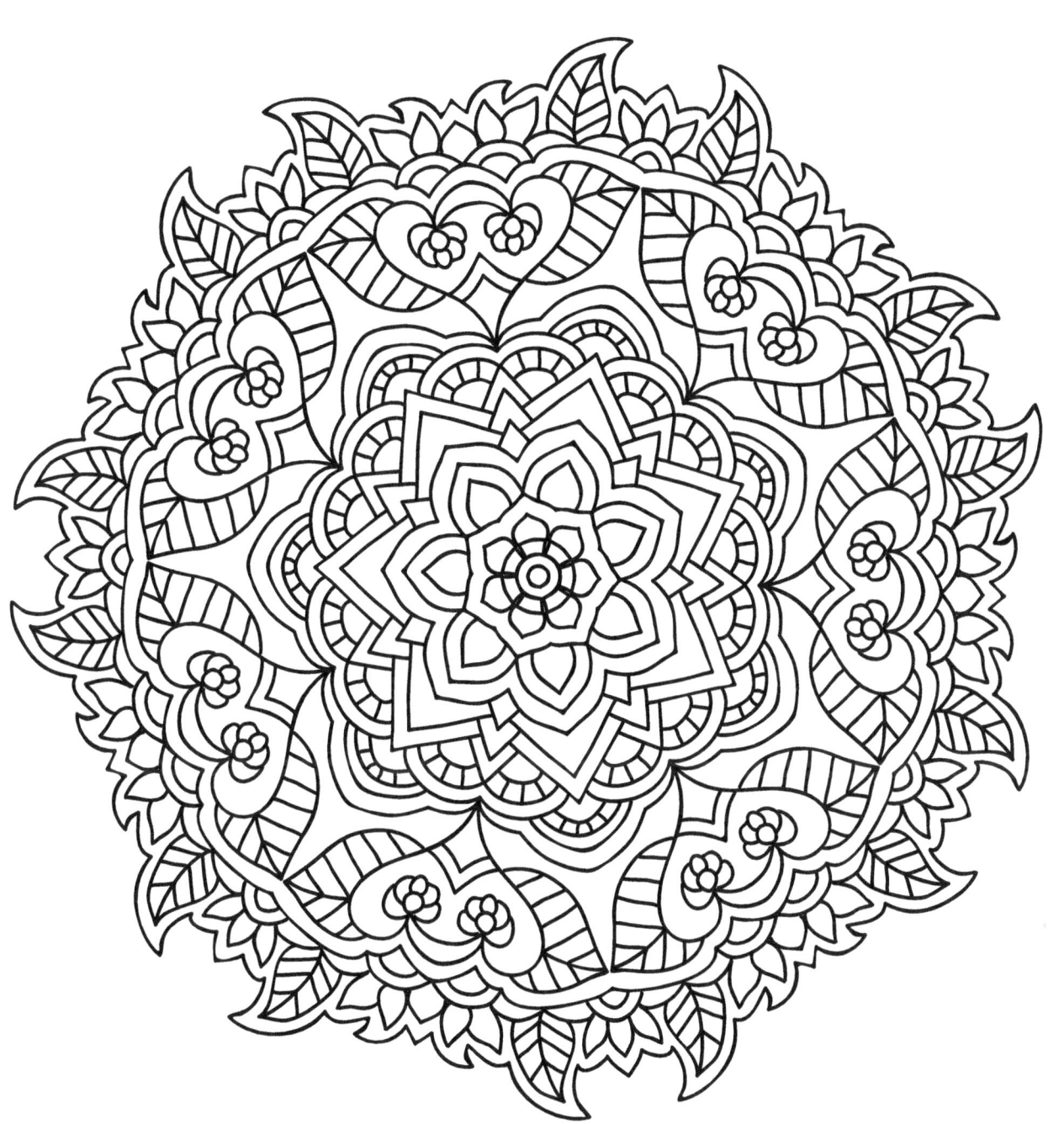

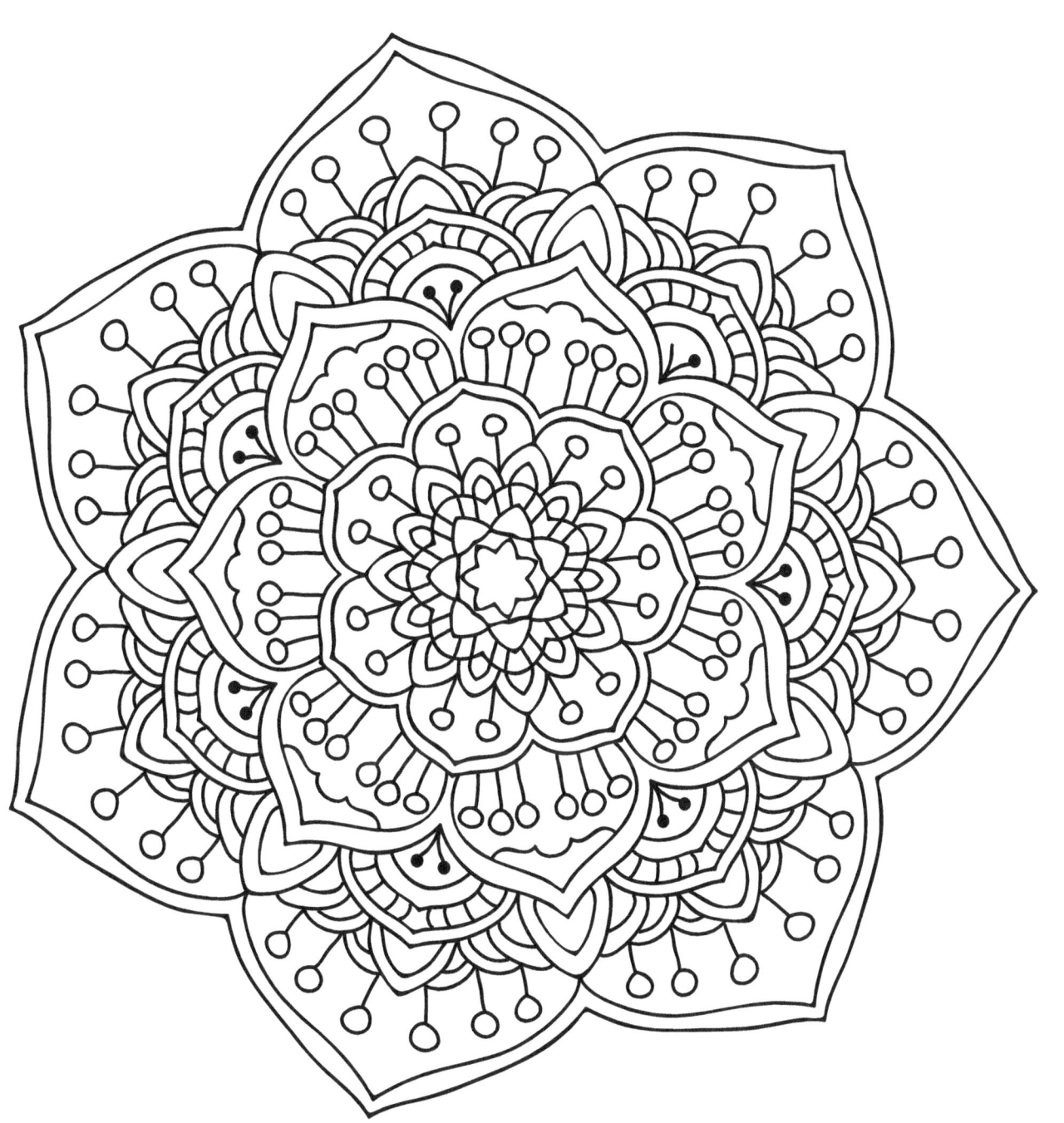

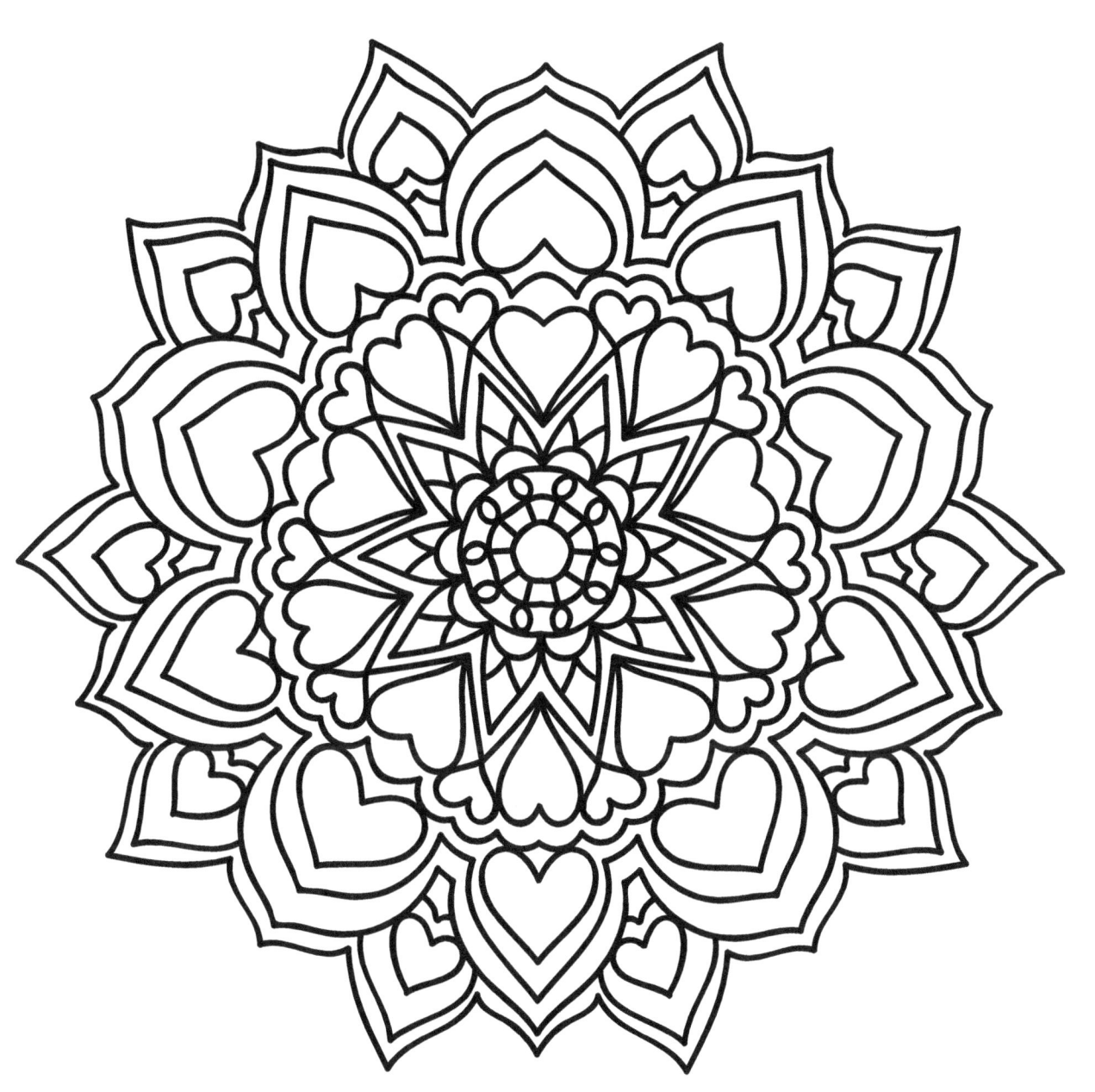

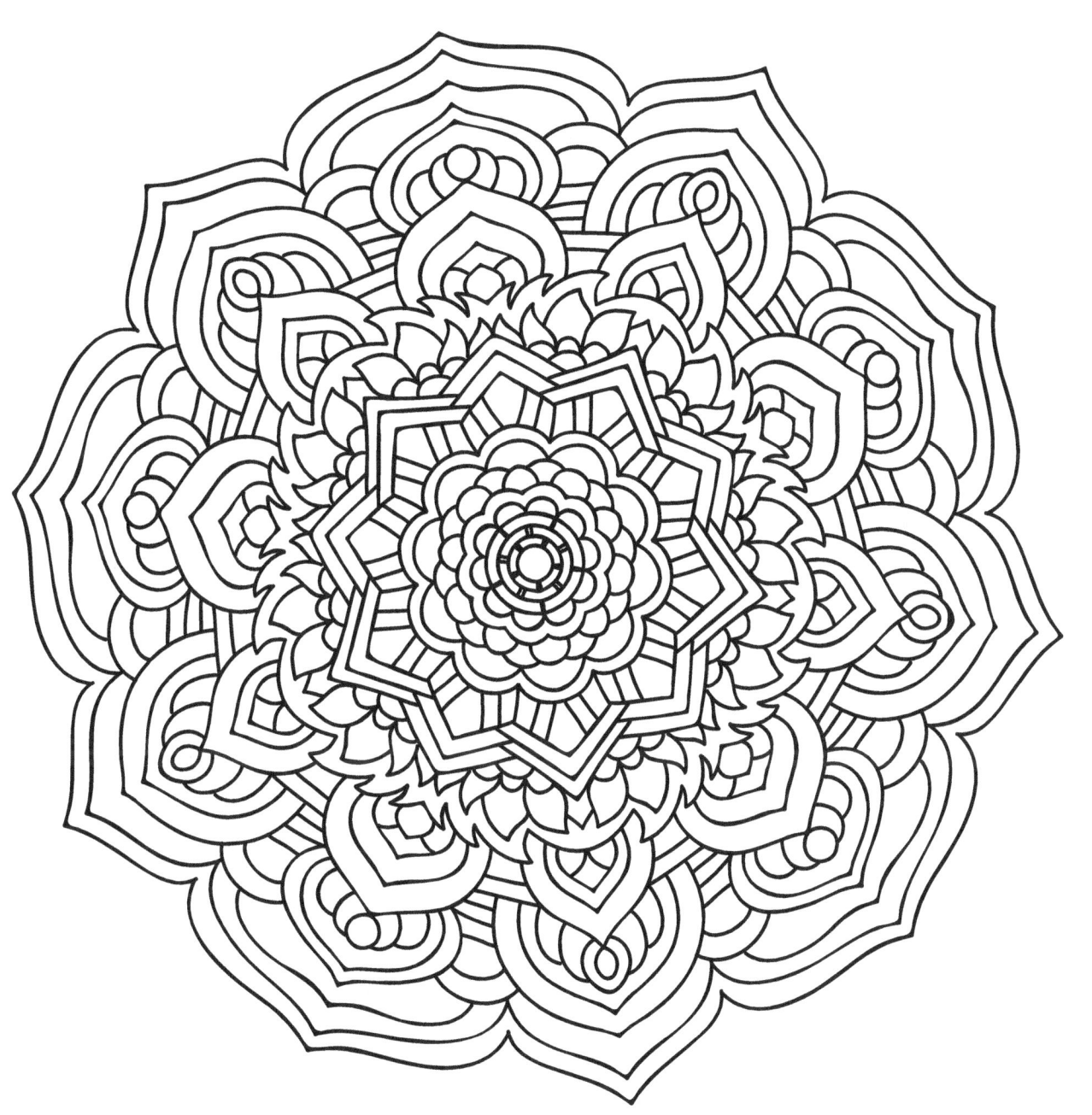

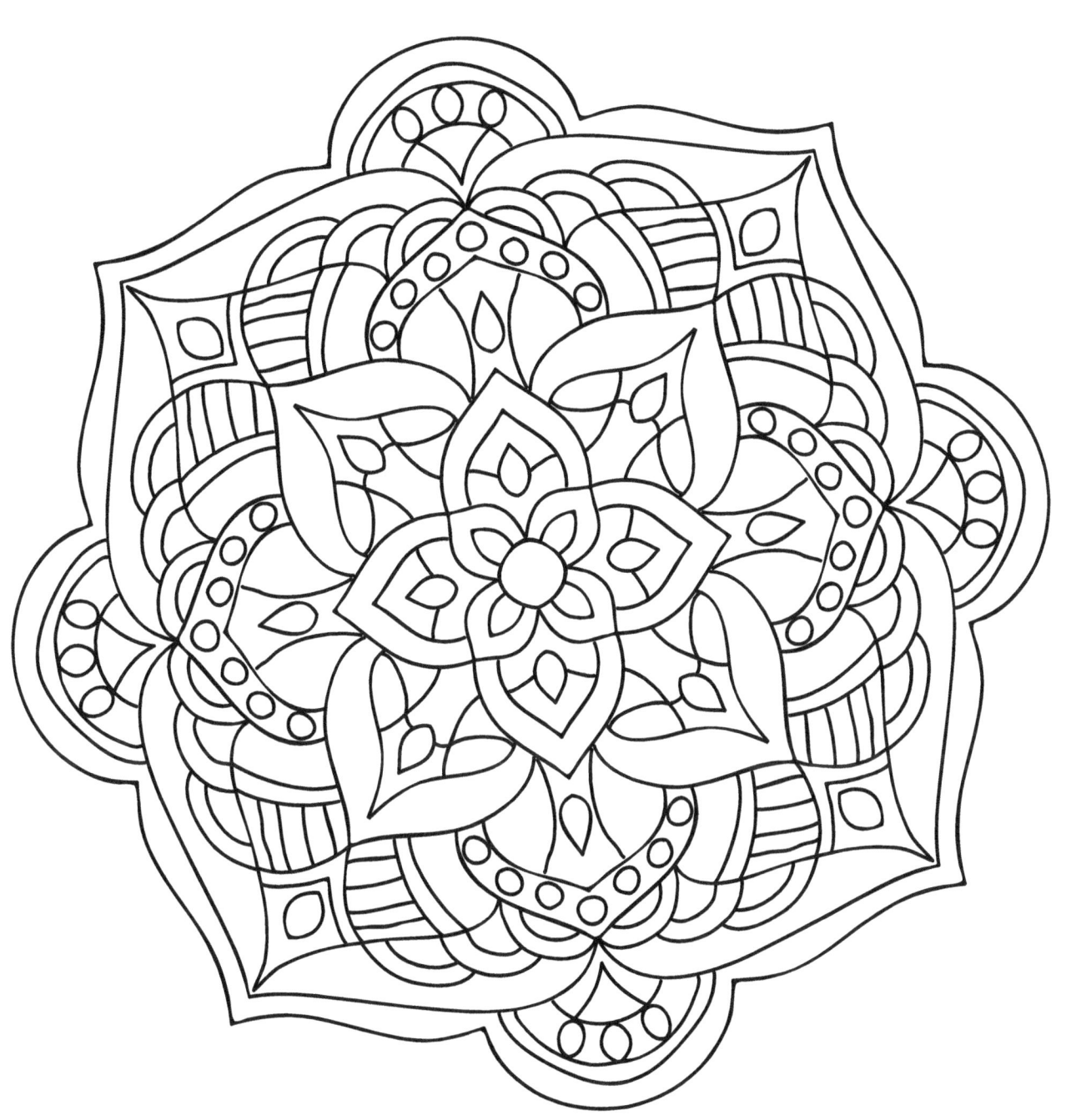

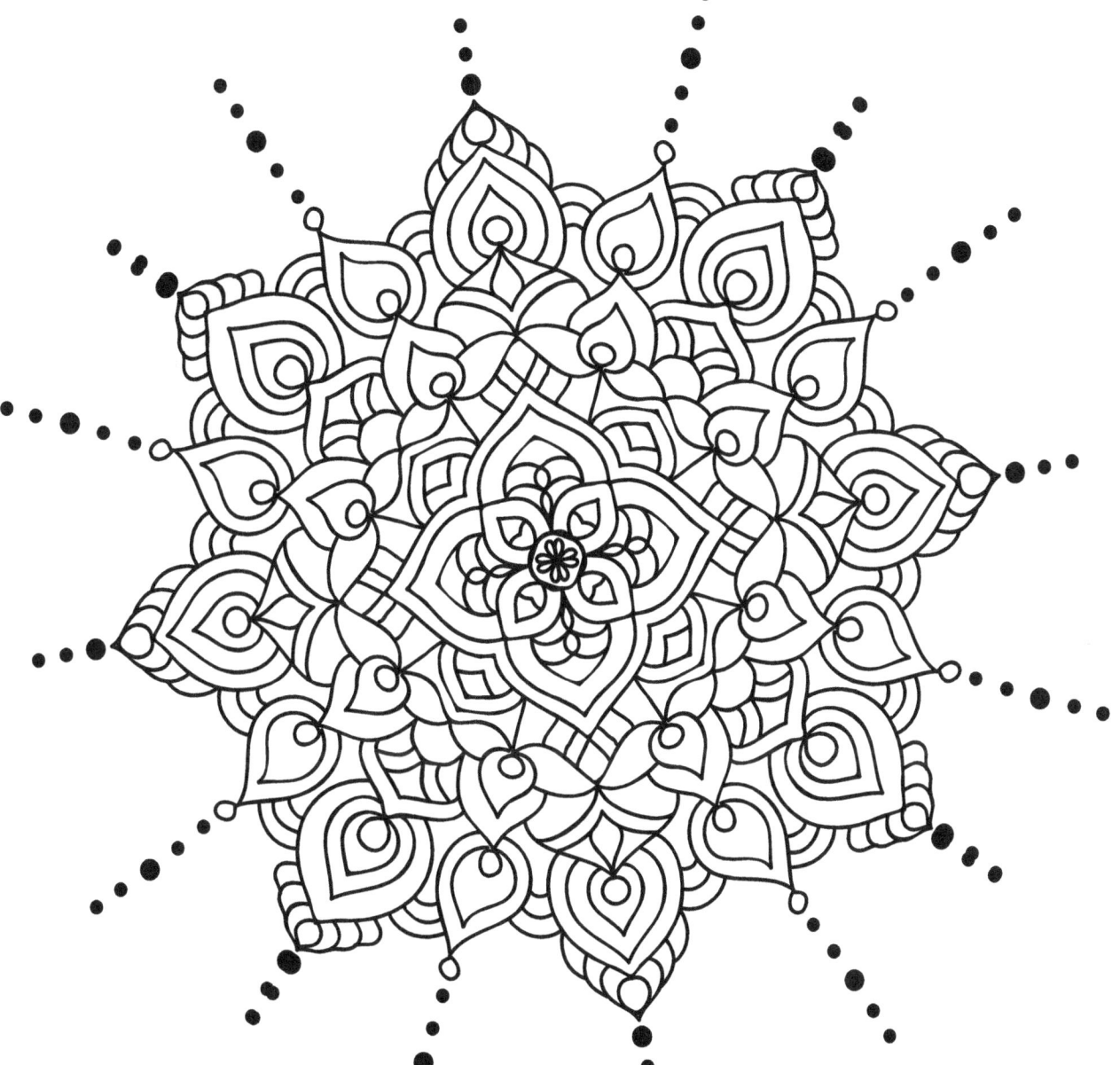

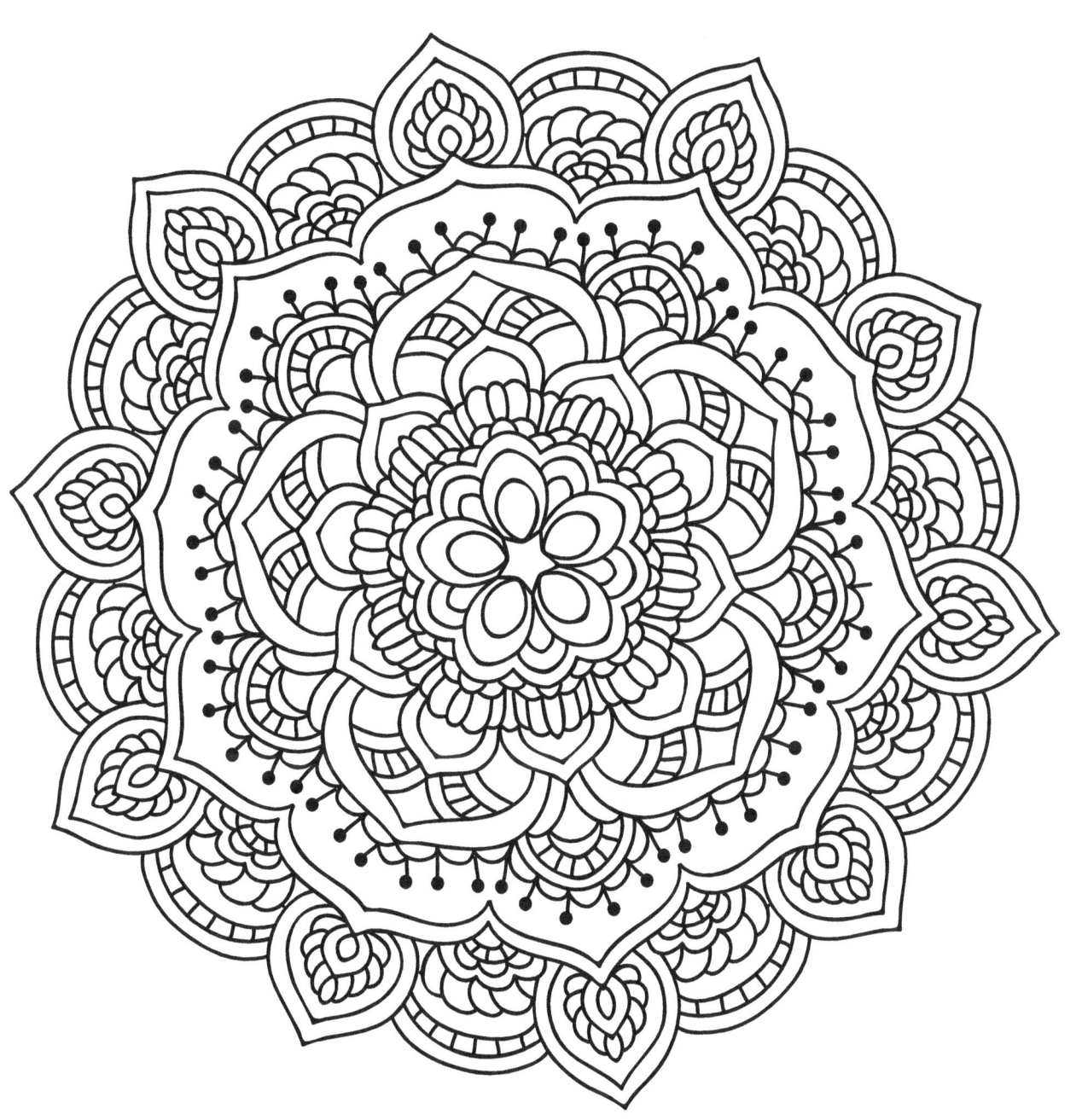

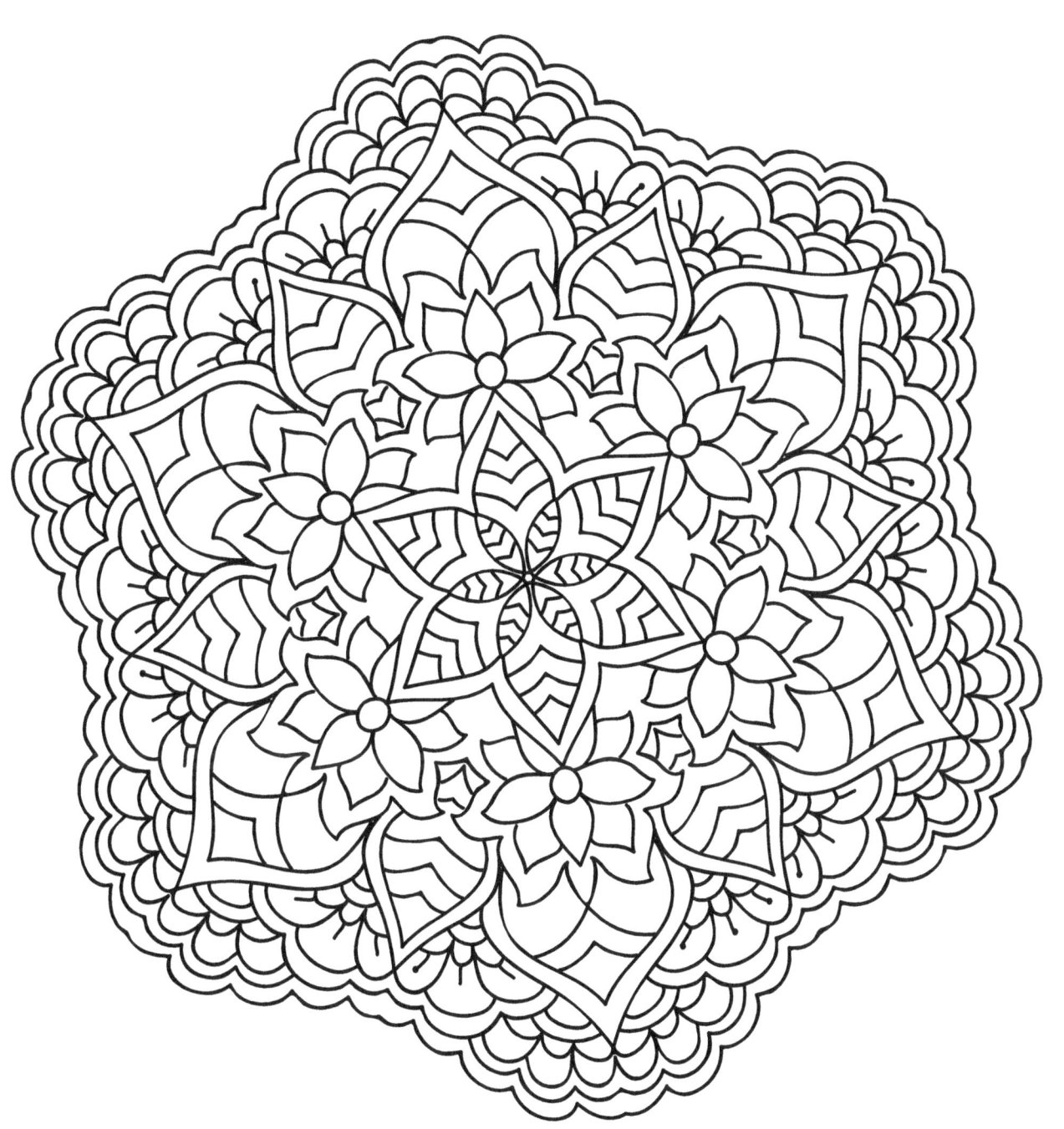

COLOR TEST PAGE

COLOR TEST PAGE

www.ingramcontent.com/pod-product-compliance
Lightning Source LLC
Chambersburg PA
CBHW060412220526
45465CB00008B/2860